HUNTER-GATHERER MORTUARY PRACTICES DURING THE CENTRAL TEXAS ARCHAIC

Texas Archaeology and Ethnohistory Series
Thomas R. Hester, Editor

Hunter-Gatherer Mortuary Practices during the Central Texas Archaic

Leland C. Bement

 University of Texas Press, Austin

Requests for permission to reproduce material from this
work should be sent to Permissions, University of Texas Press,
Box 7819, Austin, TX 78713-7819

ⓘ The paper used in this publication meets the minimum
requirements of American National Standard for Information
Sciences—Permanence of Paper for Printed Library Materials,
ANSI Z39.48–1984.

Library of Congress Cataloging-in-Publication Data

Bement, Leland C.
    Hunter-gatherer mortuary practices during the Central Texas Archaic /
Leland C. Bement. — 1st ed.
        p.   cm. — (Texas archaeology and ethnohistory series)
    Includes bibliographical references and index.

    ISBN: 978-0-292-72390-0

    1. Bering Sinkhole Site (Tex.)   2. Indians of North America—
Texas—Edwards Plateau—Funeral customs and rites.   3. Indians of
North America—Texas—Edwards Plateau—Anthropometry.   4. Indians
of North America—Texas—Edwards Plateau—Antiquities.   5. Animal
remains (Archaeology)—Texas—Edwards Plateau.   6. Plant remains
(Archaeology)—Texas—Edwards Plateau.   7. Edwards Plateau (Tex.)—
Antiquities.   I. Title.   II. Series.
E78.T4B39   1994
976.4'87—dc20   94-4789

Contents

Tables

Figures

Acknowledgments

This material is based in part upon work supported by the Texas Advanced Research Program under grant no. 003658-089 given to Solveig A. Turpin, the Cave Research Foundation, Geochron Laboratory Research Awards Program, 1991, and contributions from private individuals including August C. Bering IV, August C. Bering III, Bert Beecroft, Corbin Robertson, Mr. and Mrs. Jack B. Zilker, Mr. and Mrs. Timothy Brown, Jack and Susan Mayfield, Mr. and Mrs. Ralph Thomas, Eugene Werlin, Jr., Mrs. John C. Miller, Edward Withers, and Jesse E. Filgo. Equipment and analysis space was provided by the Texas Archeological Research Laboratory, the University of Texas at Austin.

Preface

The Edwards Plateau of central Texas is known for its long sequence of prehistoric hunter and gatherer societies. Beginning over 10,000 years ago, this band society mode persisted in central Texas until the arrival of the Spanish in the 1500s, even though neighboring groups such as the Caddoans to the east, Puebloans to the west, and Plains Villagers to the north became sedentary and adopted corn horticulture five centuries before European contact. Subsistence (procurement systems), technology, and settlement patterns of the Edwards Plateau hunter-gatherers have been reconstructed through the study of the material culture uncovered by eight decades of archaeological investigations. Missing from these reconstructions has been a study of the mortuary practices. The inability to locate more than a few burials in habitation sites or single interments under burial cairns has prevented the reconstruction of all but the most meager of burial programs. The largest number of burials from the Edwards Plateau region have been recovered by landowners excavating sediments from vertical shaft sinkholes. The commercialization of extensive cavern networks in the limestone bedrock of the region and the concentration of rich topsoils in their entrance shafts kindled a public as well as private interest in these features. Subsequent excavation of these shafts inadvertently uncovered the remains of prehistoric burials—sometimes as many as fifty individuals. Although such finds were reported to the archaeological community during the 1960s, the lack of contextual information precluded all but descriptive analysis of the retrieved skeletal remains. Thus, there has been little opportunity for systematic excavation and analysis.

This situation is compounded by the difficulty in identifying mortuary sinkholes. Sinkhole shafts are hard to find in a landscape where cracks and crevices are commonplace. When located, these sites are fraught with perils such as rattlesnakes, poisonous spiders, and precipitous entrances. Or their shafts are filled to the surface with sediments, potentially masking any evidence of their use as a burial site.

Chapter 1 presents a brief summary of the state of investigations into burial remains on the Edwards Plateau in general and in sinkholes in particular. This is followed in chapter 2 with a description of the natural and environmental setting of the site and plateau. Chapter 3, "Cultural Background and Mortuary Studies," discusses the prehistoric cultural history in the central Texas area as produced by decades of archaeological investigation. This chapter also presents various models that attempt to explain the role of mortuary practices in prehistoric hunter-gatherer societies and how their study illuminates various attributes of social structure not obtainable from the study of material culture. Chapters 4 through 8 present a description of the site, excavation procedures, and the results of the analyses of the recovered materials. The bioarchaeological analysis was conducted by three analysts working with different samples from the sinkhole. The skeletal remains initially uncovered by the track hoe and collected by the owner were analyzed by Dr. Susan McIntosh's human osteology class at Rice University (McIntosh 1988). The skeletal material recovered from the hand excavation of Units a through j were analyzed by Murray Marks, the University of Tennessee, Knoxville (Marks 1991). I performed the analysis of the osteological materials recovered by the hand excavation of Units k through o and the subsequent compilation of data presented here. Chapter 9 integrates the results of the analyses with the previously proposed models of hunter-gatherer societies and outlines a synthetic model of culture history on the Edwards Plateau during the Archaic period.

1. Introduction

Bering Sinkhole (41KR241) is a natural solution cavern, formed in the Cretaceous limestone bedrock of the Edwards Plateau in Kerr County, Texas (Figure 1), that was used by the prehistoric inhabitants of the Edwards Plateau as a repository for their dead for over 5,500 years. The material evidence gained from systematic excavation of this site supports the main premise of this study that the numerous sinkhole burial sites on the Edwards Plateau contain information about the mortuary and biological aspects of hunter-gatherer groups in Texas that, until now, has only been obtainable from the more conventional cemetery sites of the Gulf Coastal Plain.

Bering Sinkhole was discovered by a bulldozer operator clearing brush along the property line of two ranches. The sole entrance is a vertical shaft 3.8 meters long and 2.1 meters wide (Figure 2). During prehistoric times, the sinkhole was used for the disposal of human corpses by hunter-gatherer groups that frequented the drainage margin of the Johnson Fork of the Llano River. Bering Sinkhole is isolated from the habitation sites in the area. The nearest known habitation site is .75 kilometers south of the sinkhole along a major intermittent drainage. This site consists of three burned rock middens and a scatter of lithic debitage and tools. Burned rock middens are mounded concentrations of burned limestone cobbles. Such features are common on central Texas campsites. These domed accumulations vary from 25 meters squared and 50 centimeters deep to over an acre in area and 2 meters deep. Burned rock middens are thought to be the result of intensive plant-processing activities. A larger site complex of multiple large burned rock middens is located at Elm Waterhole, approximately 2.1 kilometers from the sinkhole. Surface collections of artifacts from this site indicate habitation began late in the Late Paleoindian period and continued intermittently through the Archaic and into the Late Prehistoric period. In addition to these habitation sites, the interfluves on the east, north, and south side of the sinkhole

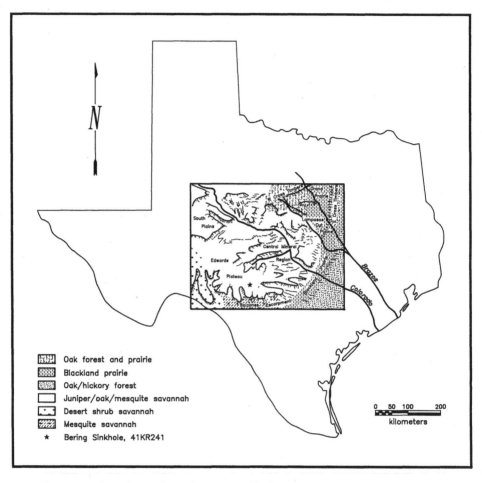

Figure 1. The relationship of Bering Sinkhole to the major physiographic and vegetational regions of Texas.

contain light scatters of lithic debitage and worked cobbles, the result of lithic procurement of the fine-grained cherts that outcrop on the hill slopes.

Sinkhole burial sites can be classified into two types: accessible and inaccessible to human traffic. In sinkholes that can be entered without ladders or ropes, burials were often interred along the walls or placed on ledges (Turpin and Bement 1988:16). In inaccessible sites, burials are found in a debris cone that developed directly under the opening as a result of natural deposition. In these cases, the dead were apparently dropped or lowered through the opening and left exposed on the underground surface. Subsequent decomposition, water action, and rodent disturbance disarticulated and distributed the skeletal re-

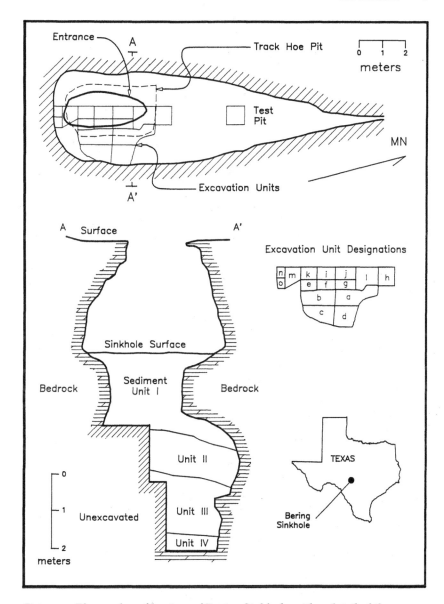

Figure 2. Plan and profile view of Bering Sinkhole with a detail of the excavation layout.

mains over the surface of the cone until they were eventually buried by sediments washed into the cavern after rains. In some instances, large limestone blocks were thrown on top of a corpse, possibly in an attempt at burial (Turpin and Bement 1988). Since the burials and accompanying grave goods are found within the natural cone beneath the opening and distributed along cone contours, it seems unlikely that the corpses were deliberately laid in place by their mourners. It cannot, however, be ruled out on the basis of the excavated materials that ladders or scaffolding of some sort were not used. The evidence does indicate that the bodies were not placed in prepared pits or sufficiently protected from the effects of rodent gnawing and water transport.

Bering Sinkhole is an example of an inaccessible sinkhole cavern used as a burial locus at various times throughout a 5,500-year span of the central Texas Archaic. At the time of discovery, a tree protruded from the entrance, and the sinkhole deposits had accreted to within 3 meters of the surface. The uppermost burial zone was buried under 2 meters of fill, and the lowest zone was under 4 meters of fill. Thus, during the time of use, the vertical drop from the surface to the floor of the cavern was between 5 and 7 meters. The recovery of all skeletal and artifactual remains from the entrance cone suggests that the bodies and offerings were simply dropped through the opening and accumulated on the talus cone below.

Logistical problems have contributed to the lack of systematic investigations in sinkhole sites including Bering Sinkhole. The vertical shaft inhibits movement of materials in and out of the cavern. Encompassing darkness, high humidity, and ambient temperatures in the 65–75 degree Fahrenheit range dictated the use of equipment more typical of mining than of archaeology. Often, the only area initially available for excavation was directly under the opening, limiting the work force to one or two until a larger area could be cleared.

In addition, the natural buildup of deposits changes the perspective offered the excavator from stacked, level deposits similar to those found in habitation sites, to canted units following the often steep-sided contours of a debris cone. Compounding this situation was the inclusion of irregularly shaped limestone blocks apparently thrown in to cover the corpses. These blocks further obfuscated the cone contours. To overcome these factors, excavation units were reduced to roughly 50-by-50-centimeter units removed in 10-centimeter-thick levels. Strike and dip measurements of long bones, artifacts, and tabular limestone blocks defined the slope of the cone surface as it changed through time and allowed the projection of that surface into adjacent excavation units. At Bering Sinkhole, four distinct and easily recognizable sediment zones provided gross checks on the contours of the cone as it was approximately 8,000, 5,100, and 3,100 years ago (see chapter 5).

The premise presented here is that Bering Sinkhole and other similar vertical shaft burial sites were used as cemeteries or communal mortuary sites and not simply as convenient single-corpse disposal areas that through time accumulated several individuals. The Bering Sinkhole analysis concentrates on reconstructing the biological, cultural, and environmental aspects of prehistoric mortuary practices of the hunter and gatherer groups of the Edwards Plateau. Specific data are sought concerning changes in aspects of the burial program, demography, and diet. These aspects are compared with data from other sinkhole sites in central Texas and the large burial sites of southeast Texas. Types of artifact classes, particularly those symbolizing a cultural referent are seriated to define shifts in social complexity as they relate to ritual activity and patterns defined at other sites. Patterns observed in the Bering Sinkhole analysis are then compared to other patterns defined in North American mortuary contexts. The burial data is then combined with previously defined cultural patterns of subsistence, technology, and social complexity to formulate a cultural synthesis for the central Texas area during the Archaic.

2. Site Setting

Bering Sinkhole (41KR241) is located on the Edwards Plateau, an up-lifted, predominantly limestone region of central Texas (Figure 1). The Edwards Plateau is the southernmost extension of the Great Plains of North America (Fenneman 1938). Contained in its 93,240-square-mile area are Cretaceous limestone and Precambrian granitic outcroppings. The Edwards Plateau is bordered on the north by the Llano Estacado and on the south and east by the western Gulf Coastal Plain. The western border is usually placed at the Pecos River, although the Stockton Plateau immediately west of the Pecos River is geologically similar and sometimes included (Gould 1975). Elevation of the Edwards Plateau ranges from 167 meters above mean sea level in the southeast along the Balcones Fault zone, to 734 meters above mean sea level along the northeastern edge. Geological and hydrological attributes accompanied by specific plant and animal communities of the Balconian biotic province make the Edwards Plateau distinct from other areas of Texas (Abbott and Woodruff 1986). The Balconian consists of few endemic species of plants or animals, but rather is a transitional area of interdigitating ranges of mesic-adapted species from the east and xeric-adapted species to the west (Blair 1950).

The central Texas cultural region includes portions of the Edwards Plateau and the Blackland Prairies, which skirt the Edwards Plateau to the east (Prewitt 1981; Figure 1). The definition of the area included in the region has been revised several times. In definitions from the late 1950s, this cultural region stretched from the Brazos River in eastern Texas to the Pecos River in southwestern Texas (Suhm 1960). The focus of this study is that portion of the culture area on the Edwards Plateau.

Geology

In the vicinity of Bering Sinkhole, the bedrock consists of the Segovia Member of the Lower Cretaceous Edwards Limestone (Barnes 1981:4).

The Segovia Member is a light gray limestone and dolomite with chert in the upper portions (Barnes 1981:4). Gray-blue and brown cherts are available in cobbles or tabular plates exposed on the surface of much of northwestern Kerr County. These medium-to-fine-grained cherts were the predominant source of siliceous material for flaked tools manufactured by prehistoric peoples in Kerr County and traded to the less endowed coastal areas. The surface exposures of limestone supplied the blocks, cobbles, and slabs used in cooking and heating fires of prehistoric groups and for making grinding implements including manos and metates.

Hydrology

The distribution and character of the water resources of the Edwards Plateau are closely tied to the geologic formations. The porous and faulted limestone makes this one of the most important aquifer regions in Texas. Surface water, originating as rain and to a lesser extent snow, is quickly channeled into the cracks and faults in the limestone and transported deep into the bedrock along water-etched passages. Deeply incised canyons and tributaries truncate the underground channels allowing the discharge of water as springs. Depending on the size of the recharge or collection area, the springs and their drainages vary from intermittent or short-term seeps to perennial streams discharging the aquifer at more constant rates (Brune 1975). The subsurface reservoirs conserve water that would otherwise be lost due to the high evapo-transpiration rates characteristic of the exposed limestone bedrock areas common to the Edwards Plateau. Conservation ensures or increases the reliability of potable water resources such as springs. Kerr County alone has fifteen of the largest springs on the Edwards Plateau (Brune 1975:49–50).

Vegetation

Today, the Edwards Plateau supports varied plant communities. The flat-to-rolling uplands are dominated by grasslands with an overstory dominated by live oak (*Quercus virginiana*), shinery oak (*Quercus havardii*), juniper (*Juniperus* sp.), and mesquite (*Prosopsis glandulosa*) and an understory of shrubs and grasses. The grasses include tall and midgrass species such as *Panicum virgatum, Sorghastrum nutans, Bothriochloa barbinodis*, and others (Gould 1975:4). The uplands consist of xeric-adapted plant species of the oak savannah. Prickly pear cactus and various yuccas hint that moisture in this setting can become scarce. Soil depth can diminish to exposed limestone bedrock. The waterways and drainages are marked by increasingly denser vegetation including an overstory of various trees and an understory of vines and shrubs. Stands of native pecans and large live oaks are found along perennial streams and rivers. In places, the deeply entrenched limestone canyons provide micro niches for ferns and mosses.

Fauna

The fauna of this region, defined as the Balconian biotic province (Blair 1950), consists of mammal species from the surrounding biotic provinces: Austroriparian to the east, Tamaulipan to the south, Chihuahuan to the west, and Kansan to the north. Mammals that range widely across the Balconian from the other provinces include *Didelphis virginiana* (opossum), *Sciurus niger* (squirrel), and *Sylvilagus floridanus* (Florida cottontail) from the Austroriparian; *Tayassu tajacu* (javelina), *Dasypus novemcinctus* (armadillo), and *Citellus mexicanus* (ground squirrel) from the Tamaulipan; *Taxidea taxus* (badger) and *Reithrodontomys montanus* from the Kansan; and *Bassariscus astutus* (ringtail), *Conepatus mesoleucus* (skunk), and *Citellus variegatus* (ground squirrel) from the Chihuahuan (Blair 1950). Other mammalian species from the various neighboring provinces have limited ranges in the Balconian. Included in this group are *Thomomys bottae* (gopher), which range eastward across half of the southern section of the province; *Sylvilagus audubonii* (desert cottontail) eastward across half the province; *Neotoma floridana* (woodrat) and *Pitymys pinetorum* (vole) extend westward halfway across the province; and *Cynamys ludovicianus* (prairie dog) enters only the northwestern quadrant of the province (Blair 1950; Hulbert 1984). The varied topography and ecological niches available on the Edwards Plateau region account for the diversity of plant and animal species seen today, and judging from the diverse species inhabiting the different areas, this was the situation prehistorically as well.

3. Cultural Background and Mortuary Studies

The central Texas culture region was defined by the distribution of a suite of artifact and site types. In recent years, as excavations progressed and site assemblages became better known, the boundaries of central Texas as a culture region were more precisely defined. According to Prewitt (1981:71), the area now stretches from Uvalde to La Grange and Temple to San Antonio.

The culture areas were not fixed on the landscape, but rather changed through time. Thus, as the chronology of the area improved, so has our understanding of the areal extent of influence by the dominant cultures through time.

Archaeological investigations of central Texas prehistoric cultures span the twentieth century. The development of Texas archaeology is characterized by two main themes of investigations: temporal and spatial. The earliest characterization of central Texas prehistory was in the form of temporal divisions developed by Pearce (1919, 1932) when he described the burned rock midden sites for the first time. He divided central Texas prehistory into three cultures based on the superpositioning of artifact assemblages found in the burned rock mounds—the characteristic site type on the Edwards Plateau. Pearce called these the lower, middle, and upper mound cultures. At the time he proposed this chronological sequence, little attention was paid to areas east and south of the Edwards Plateau where burned rock mounds were not found. Thus, the earliest reconstruction of Texas prehistory consisted of a spatially restricted site type classified by temporal subdivisions.

Following Pearce, archaeologists defined cultural assemblages for the other regions of Texas based on differences in the observed site types and artifact assemblages. These area divisions and chronologies presented Texas cultures in the terminology of the Midwestern Taxonomic system, which defines aspects and foci by temporal and spatial attributes (McKern 1939). The Pecos River Aspect was defined for the area on the western edge of the Edwards Plateau extending to New Mexico, and the Edwards Plateau Aspect consisted of components in the Edwards Plateau physiographic area (Kelley 1947, 1959).

Regional definitions culminated during the 1950s in the landmark publication of the *Handbook of Texas Archeology* (Suhm, Krieger, and Jelks 1954) in which predominantly spatial taxonomies were defined. In this study, key markers, particularly projectile points, were employed as regional indicators with broad temporal domains. The recovery of morphologically distinct projectile point forms at different levels within a site led to the development of a projectile point chronology. Generally, the oldest projectile points were lanceolate in shape. These gave way to large corner-notched and stemmed forms during the Early and Middle Archaic periods. Late Archaic projectile points were broad bladed with corner notches and expanding stems that were followed by side-notched varieties. The large dart point forms of the Archaic period were replaced by smaller arrow points of the Late Prehistoric period. Even during the Late Prehistoric, corner-notched arrow points were replaced by stemmed and unnotched forms. Assemblages, including other artifact classes, were defined that characterized each region.

During this same decade (the 1950s), the application of the newly developed technique of radiocarbon dating made it possible to sort out temporally discrete periods contained in the deposits at different sites. These cultural reconstructions continued to be represented by distinct projectile points. Thus, development of projectile point typologies continued to be in the forefront of archaeological investigations (Johnson 1964; Johnson, Suhm, and Tunnell 1962; Sorrow, Shafer, and Ross 1967).

Walter Taylor's (1948) influential conjunctive approach helped to bring about a change in archaeology by focusing attention on the context of the artifacts rather than on the artifact per se. The context included such aspects as usewear, manufacturing sequences, floral and faunal analyses, and dietary reconstructions. Weir (1976) combined the conjunctive approach with chronology building through the application of the models of cybernetics (Maruyama 1963) and equilibrium systems (Birdsell 1968) to explain cultural changes as indicated by the observed temporal changes in defined artifact assemblages and site types. Thus, within the last quarter of the twentieth century, central Texas archaeology was a mixture of chronology building, innovative studies including diet, trade, and ecology, and processual investigations of systemics.

Central Texas Chronology

One of the first central Texas chronologies was derived from the excavation of stratified sites in the Stillhouse Hollow Reservoir basin in Bell County (Sorrow, Shafer, and Ross 1967:144). The chronology, expanding an earlier construct from excavations at Canyon Reservoir in Comal County (Johnson, Suhm, and Tunnell 1962), is based on the excavations of two sites, the Landslide site and Evoe Terrace. The Landslide site contained five stratified deposits ranging in age from the late Paleoindian period (ca. 10,000 B.P.) through the Middle Archaic (ca. 3000 B.P.), with a possible minor Late Archaic component (ca. 1500 B.P.). The Evoe Terrace site contained six major components from late Paleoindian through Late Prehistoric times. Arising from these excavations was the first cultural chronology dividing the prehistoric into ten phases dating from Paleoindian through Late Prehistoric times. The Landslide site provided the definition of phases from Paleoindian through Phase VI (ca. 9000 to 3000 B.P.) and Evoe Terrace contributed corroborative data for Phases V and VI (5500 to 3000 B.P.) and then was used to define the later Phases VII–X (3000 to 500 B.P.). Major projectile point types served as temporal markers for each phase, and associated tool forms and features were provided in the strata discussions for each site.

Although the Stillhouse Hollow chronology is presented as a sequence of local phases, its correlation with the less complete sequence proposed earlier by Johnson, Suhm, and Tunnell (1962), which reflected the results of excavations of Wunderlich, Footbridge, and Oblate sites at Canyon Reservoir in Comal County, prompted Sorrow, Shafer, and Ross (1967:143) to suggest this extended chronology be applied to all of central Texas. Particular advances presented by the Stillhouse Hollow chronology include the seriation of the Early Archaic Martindale projectile point type (Hester 1971) and the Late Archaic types of Castroville, Marshall, and Fairland. Confusion of the placement of these projectile types arose from the recovery of the various types intermingled with others in sites with either deflated or shallow cultural deposits. For example, at the Youngsport site, Castroville, Montell, Ensor, and Pedernales points were recovered from the same lens with little indication of horizontal or vertical segregation (Shafer 1963). At Evoe Terrace, these point types were found in stratigraphic order with Pedernales points below Castroville and Montell (Sorrow, Shafer, and Ross 1967:144). Although the work at Stillhouse Hollow defined the relative vertical positioning of projectile point types and their associated phases, the actual age for each phase remained an estimate based on very few radiocarbon dates.

The dearth of radiocarbon dates for the central Texas region forced subsequent researchers to borrow age assignments of purported comparable deposits identified in the lower Pecos region (Weir 1976).

Shortly after Weir's presentation, the number of 14C dates from the central Texas region increased significantly, culminating in a culture chronology supported in part by a minimum of 147 assays (Prewitt 1981, 1985:202). Prewitt compiled various attributes for each phase, including site type, artifact assemblages, feature types, mortuary practices, subsistence, external relations, and age for each of thirteen phases defined for the central Texas region (Table 1). Substantial amounts of the information amassed in Prewitt's cultural chronology were obtained from the various reservoir projects in Williamson County, immediately south of Bell County, in which the Stillhouse Hollow Reservoir is located.

Extensive fieldwork conducted in Bexar County, in the southeastern portion of the Edwards Plateau, has produced another cultural chronology (Black and McGraw 1985:323). In this chronology, 12,000 years of prehistory are divided into only eleven local periods compared to Prewitt's thirteen phases. These local periods, labeled 1 through 11 (with 11 being the most recent) utilize key projectile point types as indexes.

The major differences between the Black and McGraw and Prewitt chronologies are the time boundaries for each period and the degree to which the chronology can be fine tuned. For example, Prewitt divides the Archaic into eleven phases, while Black and McGraw define seven Archaic divisions. The sequence of projectile points is similar, although many of the types used by Black and McGraw are segregated into finer periodizations by Prewitt. The controversy centers on the validity of assigning many of the types to temporally distinct periods that are combined in the Black and McGraw chronology. For example, Black and McGraw place Montell, Castroville, Marcos, and Williams dart points into local period 9, which represents the span from 650 B.C. to A.D. 250. Prewitt defines two periods within this same span: the earlier from 2600 B.P. to 2250 B.P. (600 B.C.–250 B.C.) marked by Marshall, Williams, and Lange points; and the later from 2250 B.P. to 1750 B.P. (250 B.C.–A.D. 250) marked by Marcos, Montell, and Castroville points. In short, the problem revolves around whether the archaeological record has the resolution needed to confidently segregate meaningful cultural entities across space and time to the level proposed by Prewitt. Black and McGraw maintain that the mere spatial distance across the central Texas cultural region is suffi-

Table 1 *The Correlation of Weir's (1976), Prewitt's (1985), and Black and McGraw's (1985) Chronological Sequence for the Archaic Period in Texas*

Years BP	Weir (1976) Phase	Prewitt (1985) Phase	Black and McGraw (1985) Local Period
		Toyah	11
1000		Austin	10
		Driftwood	
2000	Twin Sisters	Twin Sisters	9
		Uvalde	
	San Marcos	San Marcos	8
3000	Round Rock	Round Rock	7
		Marshall Ford	
4000	Clear Fork	Clear Fork	6
		Oakalla	
5000	San Geronimo	Jarrell	5
		San Geronimo	4
		Circleville	3
8000	Paleoindian	Paleoindian	2 & 1

ciently broad that intraregional differences are significant. They prefer local chronologies to the panregional chronology proposed by Prewitt. While Black and McGraw realize the need for developing a regional chronology, they suggest one of the type proposed by Weir (1976).

Weir's (1976:2) chronology, which we will review at some length here, is concerned primarily with the Archaic period, which it divides into five phases: San Geronimo, Clear Fork, Round Rock, San Marcos, and Twin Sisters (Table 1). The preceding Paleoindian period is characterized as a time of far-ranging groups specialized in hunting the megafauna of the terminal Pleistocene (Weir 1976:120). With the extinction of the horse, camel, mammoth, and other large herbivores, and the migration of bison from the central Texas area, Weir postulates the nomadic groups, out of necessity, adapted a hunter-gatherer lifestyle with a higher reliance on small mammals and floral species.

Beginning approximately 8,000 years ago, the hunter-gatherer groups had adapted to the changing environmental conditions and had developed a settlement/subsistence system characterized by small, widely dispersed camps seasonally occupied by small groups. Thus, the San Geronimo Phase (8000 B.P.–5000 B.P.), the first of Weir's five cultural divisions for the Archaic of central Texas, is defined.

By about 5,000 years ago, a significant change in the archaeological record occurred. Sites became more numerous, larger, contained more diverse features, and contained different lithic assemblages. Weir labeled this period of change the Clear Fork Phase (5000–4000 B.P.). Artifact diversity is comparable to that seen during the San Geronimo Phase; however, unifacial artifact intensity increases at the expense of bifaces. This shift from biface to uniface utilization is interpreted as a move toward the exploitation of specific resources. Weir suggests that during the Clear Fork Phase:

> The local group equilibrium system for this phase shifted from one of widely scattered self-sufficient nomadic bands to one with an expanded number of bands who probably participated in sharing seasonal activities. (Weir 1976:126)

The site type known as the burned rock midden appears during the Clear Fork Phase. Burned rock middens are the hypothesized aggregation sites of the seasonally congregated macrobands. Macroband aggregation would depend on the availability of high density foodstuffs such as nut crops, deer, or rabbits.

The following Round Rock Phase (4200–2600 B.P.) is characterized as an intensification of the preceding Clear Fork pattern. Burned rock midden sites accumulate at greater rates, suggesting further targeting of seasonally dense resources by macrobands. Sites are more widely distributed across the landscape, occupying a large variety of landforms from uplands to river terraces.

Two possibly coexisting settlement systems are proposed for this period. The first suggests that "macrobands, defined here as bands that significantly exceed Birdsell's modal number of 25 persons, became more common during this phase at least for a large part of the year" (Weir 1976:130). The second hypothesized settlement pattern proposes that "an increased number of smaller local groups utilized smaller territories, and each group occupied the same sites more frequently and possibly for larger periods of time" (Weir 1976:131). The proposed increase in dense floral resources, especially oak, as determined by pollen analysis, could account for the hypothesized subsistence abundance necessary to support either of these two hypotheses. The artifact assemblages define a shift toward the production of bifaces and the use of bifacial tools almost to the exclusion of unifaces. The Round Rock Phase is seen as the culmination of an economic system that began late in the San Geronimo Phase and that continued through the Clear Fork Phase. The diversity and intensity comparisons of artifacts indicate the tool assemblages were functionally more specific during the Round Rock Phase. During the Round Rock

Phase, sites are larger, contain a uniform lithic assemblage dominated by bifacial forms, and are found in almost every geographical locale, indicating a period of maximum niche utilization.

The subsequent San Marcos Phase (2800–1800 B.P.) marks the gradual decline of the consistencies seen during the Round Rock Phase. The change is perceived in the number of sites, their distribution on the landscape, and shifts in the diversity and intensity of lithic tool types. Specifically, uniface artifacts dramatically increase in diversity, and the intensity of use of all tools decreases, suggesting that the economy had become nonspecialized (Weir 1976:134). Two hypotheses are presented for the apparent change from the Round Rock Phase to the San Marcos. The first hypothesis suggests that the social system operating during the Round Rock Phase was not capable of coping with postulated increased population densities or the stresses associated with less mobile settlement patterns. The second hypothesis is that influences from the Plains, either by direct contact with Plains groups or a shift to hunting the higher number of bison entering central Texas, prompted a shift to more mobile lifeways. Whatever the impetus, the cultural remains indicate a diversification of lithic assemblages across central Texas, with cultural variability replacing the cultural homogeneity reflected in the Round Rock Phase. By the end of the San Marcos Phase, the large, burned rock middens were no longer accumulating, and there appears to be a proliferation of cultural expressions. This trend continued into the Twin Sisters Phase (2000–700 B.P.) and was accompanied by very unspecialized economies. Bison had once again become scarce in central Texas (Dillehay 1974). The Twin Sisters Phase is similar to the San Geronimo Phase in the diversity and intensity of bifacial and unifacial assemblages and in site size and distribution. Although the Late Prehistoric period (700–300 B.P.) is part of Weir's formulation, he states that the Late Prehistoric was a continuation of the patterns established during the Archaic (Weir 1976:137). Prewitt (1981:82–84) describes the Late Prehistoric as a continuation of the hunting and gathering practices of the terminal Archaic with the addition of the bow and arrow. By 650 B.P., bison once again entered the central Texas area, and hunting increased in importance (Prewitt 1981:84). In terms of group size and mobility, the San Geronimo groups were small and highly mobile bands; Clear Fork bands were larger and less mobile, at least seasonally; Round Rock groups possibly consisted of macrobands with definite seasonal aggregations of long duration; San Marcos groups were relatively smaller and more mobile; and Twin Sisters groups were once again small bands that were highly mobile.

Finally, Weir presents a three-part evolution of the central Texas Archaic cultures characterized by dissemination (dispersal) during the early Archaic, "coalescence" during the Round Rock Phase, followed by a proliferation of varied cultural groups (Weir 1976:139).

Of the various chronologies developed for the central Texas region, the one presented by Weir (1976) is used in the analysis of the sinkhole materials. Although Prewitt's (1981, 1985) chronology divides the Archaic into more time periods, its applicability to the portion of the Edwards Plateau near the sinkhole has not been tested. Black and McGraw's (1985) local chronology was not meant to be applied on a regional scale. In addition, their phases correspond closely to those proposed by Weir (1976).

The preceding environmental and cultural chronologies are based on observed changes in concrete elements whether they be pollen grains or projectile points. This is not to say, however, that these reconstructions are not open to differing interpretations. Given the principle of superposition and what is known about the biosphere, a certain factual quality has been reached in the reconstructions of the paleoenvironment and cultural assemblages. The characterization of the Archaic by Weir (1976) is based on observed changes in frequencies and forms of lithic artifacts and sites; however, much of his cultural reconstructions rely on contextual models. The following discussion presents constructs that model somewhat less tangible lines of evidence concerning the diet, health, and nutrition of prehistoric populations; the interaction between prehistoric groups, their environment, and other contemporary groups; and how these conditions and interactions changed or remained stable through time.

Review of Mortuary Studies

The multidisciplinary approach employed in the analysis of the excavated materials and geofacts from Bering Sinkhole derives from the selective use of a body of theory on sociocultural dynamics mostly relevant to band society developed up to the present. Bering Sinkhole is principally a stratified mortuary site. Synchronic studies such as Binford's (1971) approach to the study of mortuary behavior and Bartel's (1982) socioanthropological and structural applications provide viable approaches for reconstructing the social context of sinkhole use (see below). The recovery of "primitive valuables" as burial furniture suggests that Hall's (1981) import-export interaction sphere paradigm may illuminate the economic use of specific material culture items and help define extraregional contacts maintained by the hunter-gatherers utilizing the sinkhole.

For at least two decades, advances in bioarchaeological techniques, including identifying and analyzing the diet, health, and pathologies of prehistoric burial populations, have led to interpretive models of adaptive fitness through time, that is, diachronic studies (Cohen and Armelagos 1984). One model, among several to be discussed here, was developed for areas of North America with mixed deciduous forests (Dickel, Schulz, and McHenry 1984). This model traces the adaptive efficiency of hunter-gatherer groups from Archaic to Late Prehistoric times, until horticulture became a subsistence option. In this study and in others, nonhorticultural adaptations offer interesting models for the evolution of adaptive fitness on the Edwards Plateau.

The sociocultural dynamics involved in the temporal succession of hunter-gatherer groups on the Edwards Plateau has been described in terms of material culture and settlement subsistence attributes (Weir 1976; Prewitt 1981; Black and McGraw 1985; Hester 1989). Reconstructing the local paleoenvironment has relied primarily on palynology (Bryant 1977) and fauna (Toomey 1990; Dalquest, Roth, and Judd 1969; Hulbert 1984). The cultural chronologies provide the means to link the sinkhole burial groups with cultural systems over the same macro time periods (i.e., Weir's San Geronimo, Clear Fork, Round Rock, San Marcos, and Twin Sisters phases). The analyses of the Bering Sinkhole materials are placed against the backdrop of the above-mentioned mortuary models. In addition, the Bering Sinkhole data will be incorporated into the reconstructed cultural sequence proposed by Weir (1976).

Interpretive Models

The study of mortuary practices consists of the reconstruction of the biological variables, including age, sex, and inherited traits, and cultural variables, including grave placement, grave morphology, corpse processing, and grave furnishings. The identification of patterns in the biological and cultural variable sets defines a specific burial program for a given society within one macro time frame (i.e., the San Geronimo Phase). Following are various models that utilize mortuary site and burial program data. Some of these models, employing similar data sets, construct diametrically opposed cultural systems. Throughout this book, I have tried to refrain from using the term "cemetery" to describe mortuary sites, since this term often denotes sedentism and complex society. However, various archaeologists throughout North America use "cemetery" when referring to discrete areas set aside by a hunter-gatherer or agricultural society for the sole purpose of interring the dead. The term "cemetery" is used to describe the mortuary sites of certain hunter-gatherer groups as they have been defined in North American archaeology (Charles and

Buikstra 1983:119; Dickel, Schulz, and McHenry 1984). In these instances, "cemetery" refers to a mortuary site separated from the areas of everyday activity. This use of "cemetery" does not follow that used by urbanists in which cemeteries are functionally linked to densely populated areas (Schaedel 1991). Other terminology that is avoided here, except in reference to its use by others, is sedentary hunter-gatherers. In this use, sedentary refers to semisedentary or quasi-sedentary mobility patterns wherein macrobands at base camp settlements are annually inhabited by at least some members of the group, for example, the aged (Charles and Buikstra 1983:126).

Binford (1971) discusses the history of archaeological investigations in mortuary practices. Through use of intercultural comparisons, he dispels the idealist assumption "that cultural variations resulted from either differential intellectual creativity or differential lineal transmission and/or intergroup communication of ideas" (Binford 1971:15) and Kroeber's propositions that mortuary practices are unstable, variable, and not integrated with the rest of society. In refuting Kroeber's (1927) proposition that mortuary practices were a separate entity not contained in the "core" of the cultural system, Binford demonstrates by use of ethnographic records that differences in mortuary rites are linked to differences in group affiliation and "social organizational features" (1971:14). Thus, complexity and differentiation in burial modes and furnishings reflect the compartmentalization of distinct social personas in the societal structure. Hypothetically, burial modes vary according to the deceased's "(1) age, (2) sex, (3) relative social status within the social unit, and (4) social affiliation in membership units within a society or in the society itself" (Binford 1971:15).

In addition, Binford divides mortuary rites into technical and ritual components.

> Technically, burial customs provide for the disposal of the potentially unpleasant body of the deceased. Ritually, mortuary rites consist of the execution of a number of symbolic acts that may vary in two ways: in the form of the symbols employed, and in the number and kinds of referents given symbolic recognition. (Binford 1971:16)

The form and structure of the mortuary rites vary according to the form and complexity of the structural characteristics of the society. Thus, the number of referents given symbolic recognition should equate to the number of potential positions contained in the societal structure. The individual's social persona, "the composite of the social identities held in life" (Binford 1971:19), provides the criteria for determining the mortuary treatment accorded at death. In hunter-gatherer societies, the potential number of social positions is relatively fewer than in more complex societies, and it usually varies according to age, sex, and personal achievement.

According to Binford, two phenomena could be symbolized in the mortuary practices: (1) that accorded the social persona of the deceased and (2) that which identifies the social group corresponding to the structural level of the social persona. It is, after all, the living who bestow the rites on the dead. Binford's (1971:23) cross-cultural analysis concludes "that the form and structure which characterize the mortuary practices of any society are conditioned by the form and complexity of the organizational characteristics of the society itself." At Bering Sinkhole, then, various attributes of the society may be indicated by differential treatment of the dead through preburial handling or associated grave goods. Although a one-to-one correlation between grave goods and specific individuals may not be possible, overall qualitative changes through time may indicate changes in the social structure.

Bartel (1982:54), like Binford (1971), reviews the archaeological analysis of mortuary practices that he characterizes as an inverse black box relationship. The classic black box consists of the sequence where known input acts on an unobservable object to produce an observable output. For archaeologists, such known inputs include environmental and biological factors. The unknown object is the social structure, and the observable output is the archaeological remains. Mortuary practices, however, are an inverse black box where the input (social relationships of living participants) is unobservable, and it acts on the object, in this case corpse disposal that is observable, to produce an unobservable output including the postmortem behavior of the living (Bartel 1982:54). Archaeologists, through the use of ethnographic analogy, can sometimes crack the inverse black box and shed light on the usually unobservable input and output stages due to redundancies in correlations of aspects of the burial sequence. One such correlation between the observable corpse disposal and unobservable social relationship is found in the recovery of burial furnishings that symbolize various social referents (persona) such as status, economic exchange, and social structure (Binford 1971).

> Thus, it seems that the archaeologist can make the operational assumption that explanation and postdiction about social dimensions can be made solely from corpse disposal. (Bartel 1982:55)

Aside from reflecting the internal structuring of societies, mortuary practices have been used to model intergroup relations.

Mortuary practices have also been studied for their role in the establishment and maintenance of social relationships between and within corporate groups (Bloch and Parry 1982; Jirikowic 1990). These studies explore the power or political implications of death and the reestablishment of the social system through negotiated relations secured during corporate group aggregation for mortuary rituals. The burial program acknowledges the death of the individual but then emphasizes the regeneration of the social order through the reapportionment of the deceased's social alliances.

This line of investigation, developed by ethnographers, has only recently been applied to archaeological materials (Jirikowic 1990). Here, emphasis is placed on the social relations aspects of the mortuary program. Differently applied burial attributes such as cremation, bundling, primary burial, inclusion of furnishings, and the like, are not viewed as reflecting the different social personae of the deceased. Instead, a social reason defined at a level above that of the individual is invoked so that different treatments could be applied to the same person or social persona. Thus, the situation of death, in its relation to an event such as corporate aggregation, could dictate whether an individual receives cremation, primary burial followed by bundling, or primary interment at the corporate aggregation site (Hertz 1960; Jirikowic 1990).

Such a study proved fruitful in the analysis of ossuary sites of historic and protohistoric Huron groups in the northeast United States (Jirikowic 1990). The ossuaries in Jirikowic's study contained cremations, bundles, and articulated inhumations in the same communal burial pit. Through the inferences based on ethnohistorical accounts, she proposed that the ossuary-type final burial corresponded with the cyclical occurrence of the Feast of the Dead. This ceremony (which was recorded as having been performed at intervals ranging from 1 to 8 years) required the presence of the remains of everyone who had died since the last ceremony. The differential treatment of the corpses found in the ossuary was interpreted as a functional response by the prehistoric Huron to the scheduling of the next ceremony. Cremation or burial followed by bundling would have been practiced if the next ceremony was in the distant future, and primary inhumation would have been performed on anyone who died immediately prior to the Feast of the Dead.

The primary theme of the Huron study centered on the social interactions conducted during corporate group aggregation. Ritual affirmation of the deaths served to inform anyone in the corporate group that had not already known (which is highly unlikely) that a member had died, thus opening any negotiated ties to redistribution to other members of the society. Hence, exchange alliances held by the deceased were renegotiated among his relatives or otherwise reapportioned. In this fashion, the social structure of intercorporate and intracorporate group interactions was maintained or, in terms of death and fertility, reproduced.

Thus, it is seen that the dead were ritually acknowledged, and social obligations and affiliations were open for renegotiation or reproduced among the living. At death, the social obligations and alliances of the deceased were suspended or were no longer held binding or sanctioned by the corporate group. However, at a designated social event, such as the Feast of the Dead, any renegotiated alliances or obligations received social recognition and sanctification. The new social order was likewise made public to all members of the corporate group, so that everyone had the information necessary to act in the socially prescribed way. Thus, the social structure hypothetically would have been reproduced.

Not all groups designated specific areas for burials. Ethnographic studies of African hunter-gatherer groups describe rituals related to the dead that are conducted at aggregation sites located away from the actual burial sites. In Woodburn's (1982) account of the mortuary programs for four African hunter-gatherer societies, the dead are buried within their residences and then the hut is pulled down on top when the group moves on. This is the immediate action taken upon a death. However, when the band got together at the seasonal aggregation site, one of the rituals offered recognition to all members of the corporate group who had died since the last aggregation (Woodburn 1982). These rituals illustrate this practice of delayed death recognition that is followed by the reintegration of the members of the corporate group and the reestablishment of social ties and alliances held by the deceased persons. That the same social negotiations transpired at corporate aggregations, even though the actual burials were dispersed across the landscape, such as that described by Woodburn (1982), is the point of Bloch and Parry's (1982) emphasis on the reproduction of the social order regardless of the final disposition of the dead.

That mortuary sites have other cultural purposes is shown by Goldstein (1980), who proposes that sedentary horticulturists used burial facilities as a display of territorial ownership for the control of key resources. In these instances, the mortuary sites provided an ancestral or lineal legitimization of ownership. A variation of this model has been applied to the Archaic hunter-gatherer mortuary sites found in the middle Mississippi River drainage of North America (Charles and Buikstra 1983).

In this instance, the burial site is hypothesized as the symbol, and the corporate group is the referent. By extension, the territory around the mortuary facility would be claimed by the corporate group that utilized the locus. Inclusion in the burial area equated to inclusion in the corporate group (Binford 1971).

Charles and Buikstra (1983:119) provide four postulates for the correlation of discrete burial loci (termed "cemeteries" by Charles and Buikstra) and lineal corporate groups:

Utilization of formal cemetery areas will correlate with sedentary subsistence strategies employed by the group(s) using the cemetery.

The degree of spatial structuring present in the mortuary domain will correlate with the degree of competition among groups for crucial resources.

Within the larger society, corporate groups will be distinguished by inclusion in separate cemeteries or in spatially distinct areas within a single cemetery.

Inclusion of individuals in the cemetery implies inclusion of those individuals in the corporate groups. (Charles and Buikstra 1983:119, 120)

Charles and Buikstra acknowledge the difficulty in modeling mortuary behavior from a cross-cultural framework and proceed to demonstrate the utility of their model in a regional study. Rather than predicting or establishing the level of competition for crucial resources between corporate groups, they use a diachronic scale of intensity. By this means, they are able to demonstrate that at various times in the cultural sequence, corporate group competition intensified or lessened. By limiting the study to a restricted region, they evoke tradition (as determined by archaeological investigation) to provide a cultural "inertia" in which social and cultural changes develop by altering components of the previously existing status quo (Charles and Buikstra 1983:125). The element of tradition provides a basic backdrop of cultural systems including the development of adaptive technologies and

. . . change will involve modifications of previously existing patterns. A representation system, such as a set of mortuary practices, should change as the set of phenomena it is representing changes or as the significance of those phenomena changes. (Charles and Buikstra 1983:125)

Charles and Buikstra use the above formulation in the analysis of Archaic pre-Titterington and Titterington-like mortuary sites in the middle Mississippi River drainage. They show an association between large base camps and hilltop cemeteries and infer that the burials may have legitimized control of subsistence resources within a defined territory by establishing ownership through direct lineal descent ties with ancestors.

Privileges afforded members of the corporate group would include rights to the crucial, highly valued nut and deer resources and burial in the designated area. Corporate membership for adults relied on their participation in subsistence tasks. Infants and children were accorded membership as an extension of their adult kindred status.

Charles and Buikstra were able to show an increase through time in the consistency in form of mortuary sites, and they link this increase to the heightened competition between corporate groups for crucial subsistence resources. As competition increased in the main river valleys, spin-off corporate groups moved into the less, yet still adequate, productive tributary valleys.

The use of the term "sedentary" by Charles and Buikstra is perhaps a poor choice of terminology, especially when describing hunter-gatherer societies. In the first place, sedentary equates to year-round occupancy of a site. This clearly is not what is meant by Charles and Buikstra as is evident by their use of "sedentary" to refer to large, repeatedly occupied base camp settlements that may be annually inhabited by some members of the group (i.e., aged) and that can include a "seasonal round contained within a stable territory" (Charles and Buikstra 1983:126). The degree of mobility included in their definition is further indicated in the following passage that discusses the use of cemeteries in the areas near secondary streams where subsistence distribution was not as concentrated as that seen along the major river valleys (Charles and Buikstra 1983:132).

The populations occupying the smaller secondary drainages, where the resources were more dispersed, would have ranged over wider areas during their seasonal rounds than would those populations inhabiting the major valleys, with their characteristic closely packed environmental zones. In the latter areas, the dominance of primary interments implies that death usually occurred at a location within close proximity to the cemetery, indicating little utilization of resource exploitation sites at any great distance from the burial site. On the other hand, the very high frequency of bundle burials and disarticulated remains at the sites in the tributary valleys may indicate that most deaths occurred at such a distance from the interment facility that the bodies required processing and storage at the occupied location until final burial could be completed when the seasonal round brought the group near the cemetery. (Charles and Buikstra 1983:132)

Thus, the term "sedentary" means anything but nonmobile in its use by Charles and Buikstra, and the burial locality is more aligned with a planned seasonal stop at an important cultural site.

The purposeful repeated scheduling of a return to a site as a specific stop in a seasonal round, especially if the site's primary importance is for reasons other than subsistence activities, is a defining characteristic of a pattern of cyclical nucleation at a cultural shrine (Schaedel 1991). Cyclical nucleation at a mortuary site, described by Charles and Buikstra (1983) as the seasonal return to the cemetery, provides a predominantly social reason for the scheduled stop. This is reminiscent of the Huron Feast of the Dead locale (Jirikowic 1990) and ethnographic descriptions of delayed recognition of the dead in certain African hunter-gatherer societies (Woodburn 1982). Such a situation could allow for a longer interval between scheduled stops at the burial ground than the usual seasonal time frame inherent in subsistence scheduling. Thus, the pattern of burial facility use described by Charles and Buikstra (1983) could be explained by a hunter-gatherer model of cyclical nucleation at a burial site or shrine, or both.

Base camp settlements, as opposed to a residential mobility settlement pattern, form the basic dichotomy in the proposed model of settlement patterns on the Edwards Plateau (Gunn and Mahula 1977). Gunn (1977) observes that subsistence resource densities on the Edwards Plateau varied according to broad meteorological gradients that crossed the Edwards Plateau from east to west. He then postulates that prehistoric hunter-gatherer group mobility patterns could be modeled after subsistence resource density. Gunn proposes that periods of ameliorated environmental conditions were more conducive to base camp settlements—termed transhumant settlement— and harsher environments prompted a residential mobility pattern— termed nomadic pattern (Gunn 1977). In this model, as temperature and effective moisture patterns changed, the settlement pattern shifted between a nomadic system of residential mobility to a less mobile system of base camp settlements (later defined as logistic mobility by Binford 1980). In the transhumant or logistic pattern, the band inhabited a base camp for an extended period of time, usually several seasons, and task groups composed of a subset of the residential population conducted logistical forays to obtain subsistence items. Thus, the base camp was located in an area from which numerous, seasonally available foodstuffs could be obtained without the need of moving the band. In the nomadic system, the residential group moved from camp to camp, foraging the nearby area for subsistence items. In this system, the band usually consisted of a smaller population than that allowed by the less mobile transhumant system (Gunn 1977; Binford 1980). Although this model includes aspects of environmental determinism, the correlation between major environmental shifts in temperature and moisture and cultural variation through adaptation cannot be overlooked (Bryant and Shafer 1977).

Changes in mobility patterns are often accompanied by shifts in certain biological factors (Cohen and Armelagos 1984). Among these are changes in fertility, nutritional levels, stress levels, and disease. Models of the association of these attributes to changes in settlement systems have been formulated for hunter-gatherer groups in the Mississippi River valley and central California region (Dickel, Schulz, and McHenry 1984; Rose et al. 1984).

Dickel, Schulz, and McHenry (1984), working with central California hunter-gatherer mortuary populations, construct a model of prehistoric adaptation from approximately 4500 B.P. through protohistoric times. They investigate the bioarchaeological aspects of stress associated with the elaboration of diets centered on acorns. The cultural system evolved from a hunting-oriented subsistence pattern with little reliance on acorn/vegetal foodstuffs to a strict reliance on acorns supplemented by hunting and fishing. The early diet was high in protein and low in carbohydrates; whereas during the later period, the people subsisted on a diet high in carbohydrates and low in protein. Accompanying the shift in emphasis toward a storable staple diet of acorns was increased population density (along with increased population size), reduced mobility, increased interpersonal conflict, reduced seasonal nutritional stress, and increased chronic stress. Social complexity increased, supposedly in response to the increase in the band size, and is reflected in the mortuary data by an increase in status-related grave furniture (King 1978).

Indicators employed to track changes in the populations included pathologies related to the nutritional and stress load reflected in the mortuary populations. Dental hypoplasias were used as an indicator of chronic stress, whereas Harris lines indicated seasonal stress. Overall nutrition level was characterized by the rates of dental caries and abscesses, and infection rates were indicated by pathologies of the bone.

The study of the California groups concluded that the earlier periods were characterized by small group size and high mobility patterns, a diet high in protein and low in carbohydrates, and high seasonal stress as indicated by high Harris line rates and low hypoplasia rates. The later groups with a higher population density followed a seasonally sedentary pattern, subsisted on a diet low in protein and high in carbohydrates, and suffered from high chronic stress as indicated by high hypoplasia rates and low Harris line rates.

Comparative Texas Mortuary Sample

Large mortuary sites containing individual interments of flexed or extended corpses, cremations, or bundles have been identified in the Gulf Coastal Plain to the east and south of the Edwards Plateau (Hall 1981; Lukowski 1988). This portion of the state, distinguished as southeast Texas (Hall n.d.:1), has yielded burial populations dating from the Middle Archaic to Historic Indian times (Reinhard, Olive, and Steele 1989). Of 25 components in 20 Archaic burial sites, only 2 are Middle Archaic, 9 Late Archaic, and 14 Late Prehistoric. Burial numbers range from 10 at the Green Lake site (Wingate and Hester 1972:119–127) to over 300 at Morhiss (Duffen 1939; Hall n.d.:8). The southeast Texas mortuary sample has been summarized as follows (Hall n.d.:29):

> The area contains most of the known Archaic cemeteries in the state. Certain of the cemeteries in the group have yielded the largest mortuary populations presently known.

> From only two known cemeteries in the Middle Archaic, there is a dramatic increase in cemetery numbers after 500 B.C., this development continuing on through the Late Prehistoric period.

> Graves in Late Archaic cemeteries, representing the period from 500 B.C. to A.D. 300, are lavishly furnished in comparison to Middle Archaic and Late Prehistoric graves found throughout the same area. Some of the artifacts found in the Late Archaic graves come from at least as far away as the Ouachita Mountains in west central Arkansas and perhaps also from the coasts of Alabama or Florida.

The following mortuary sites have yielded data that will be compared to the burial levels at Bering Sinkhole. The Ernest Witte site (41AU36) is located on a bluff overlooking Allens Creek, a tributary of the Brazos River (Hall 1981). This site yielded an estimated 238 burials in 4 discrete burial levels dating from Middle Archaic to Late Prehistoric times. The earliest group, Burial Group 1, contained an estimated 60 primary burials and 1 cremation. Over 80 percent of the burials were of adults, and less than 20 percent were of subadults. Most of the primary burials had extended body positions. Grave goods found with 7 of the primary burials consisted of 1 Pedernales dart point and 3 types of pointed bone artifacts. Burial Group 2, assigned to the Late Archaic, contained 140 primary interments, 3 cremations, and 2 bundle burials. Almost 75 percent of the burials were adults, and 25 percent were subadults. As with Group 1 burials, the bodies of the majority of the primary interments were in an extended position. Grave furnishings were recovered from 70 burials, both male and female, and both bundle burials. The burial goods consisted of dart points, marine shell ornaments, corner-tang knives, boatstones, ground stone gorgets, graphite schist abraders, red jasper pebbles, ocher, biotite schist, bone artifacts, and deer skulls and antlers (Hall 1981:273).

Burial Group 3 contained 10 individuals, including 6 semiflexed, 1 flexed, and 3 who were either extended or whose position was not determined. Eight of the 10 burials were adults. The 1 grave with burial goods held 7 Godley dart points, a transitional Archaic style. None of the 13 burials in Group 4 were accompanied by artifacts. The burials consisted of 9 adults and 4 subadults. Eight of the bodies were semiflexed, and 3 were flexed.

The mortuary component at Ernest Witte provided a diachronic pattern of use from the Middle Archaic through the Late Prehistoric. Of particular importance was the high number of burials from the Late Archaic compared to those for the Middle Archaic or subsequent transitional Archaic and Late Prehistoric periods. Accompanying the increased use was an increase in extraregional contacts with areas far to the east and northeast, specifically Arkansas and Florida (Hall 1981:303).

Loma Sandia, in Live Oak County, is located between the Edwards Plateau and the Gulf of Mexico. This site, dated to the terminal Middle Archaic, yielded 110 interments, including at least 4 cremations (Taylor and Highley n.d.:1399). Most of the bodies were flexed or tightly flexed, and burial goods were recovered from 96 graves. Grave goods included projectile points, thin bifaces, cores, beveled tools, hammerstones, ground stone, asphaltum, bone tools, deer antler racks, shark teeth, marine shell ornaments, and freshwater mussel shells. No evidence of far-reaching trade such as that described at Ernest Witte was recovered, but several caches of large bifaces suggest exchange of high-quality cherts with the Edwards Plateau region.

At the Olmos Dam site (41BX1) along Olmos Creek at the eastern edge of the Balcones Fault zone, 13 flexed primary burials and 1 possible bundle burial were recovered (Lukowski 1988). This mortuary site is assigned to the Late Archaic, based on cultural associations and broad radiocarbon dates. Deer antlers were recovered from 7 of the 13 burials. Other grave goods included marine shell ornaments, freshwater mussel shells, ocher, large chert cobbles, worked bone including tubular bone beads, ground stone, and worked stone artifacts. Again, no evidence of trade with groups from the southeastern United States was found.

Each of these sites also contained evidence of habitational debris. However, in all cases, the burials were placed away from the habitation or midden areas.

In addition to these mortuary sites on the coastal plain, a number of sinkholes on the Edwards Plateau and in areas of western Texas have produced burials (Turpin and Bement 1988). Seminole Sink (41VV620) is the only sinkhole in Texas that has received excavation and analysis comparable to that accorded the large mortuary sites such as Ernest Witte and Loma Sandia (Turpin 1988). This site, located in Seminole Canyon in the lower Pecos region, produced the remains of 21 early Archaic individuals and 1 proto-Historic cremation. The only prehistoric artifact was an early corner-notched dart point. This projectile point and radiocarbon dates of sediments place the early Archaic use between 6800 and 5300 years B.P. Bioarchaeological analysis described a population well adapted to their environment. Low levels of childhood stress, anemia, and minor trauma were identified (Marks, Rose, and Buie 1988). High caries rates and early tooth loss were attributed to a diet high in fiber and carbohydrates. Tooth wear patterns indicated that deaths during all seasons of the year were represented (Marks, Rose, and Buie 1988).

Two other sinkholes, Mason Ranch in Uvalde County and Hitzfelder Cave in Bexar County, yielded in excess of 25 burials each. Mason Ranch Sinkhole produced an estimated 25 to 50 individuals from a shaft 11 meters deep (Benfer and Benfer 1981). Burial goods included Travis, Nolan, and Tortugas dart points. Hitzfelder Cave yielded between 30 and 50 burials along with bone awls, bone beads, freshwater mussel shells, and dart points including 3 Frio, 1 Pedernales, and 1 Marshall/Lange (Givens 1968; Collins 1970). Neither of these sites was excavated professionally, and only cursory analysis of the remains has been accomplished.

Cueva de la Candelaria in the Laguna district of northern Mexico produced unparalleled information on sinkhole use due to extraordinary preservation of perishable materials (Aveleyra, Maldonado, and Martinez 1956). This site, roughly assigned to the Late Prehistoric period, yielded tightly flexed burials wrapped in numerous mats and robes and bound with twine or hair ropes. Elaborate burial furnishings included engraved gourd jugs, hafted knives, beaded rattles, rattlesnake vertebra necklaces, cradles, and numerous items of personal adornment. A single dog burial was also recovered. Evidence for such preburial treatment is not preserved in the wet caves of the Edwards Plateau.

The following chapters present the results of the analyses of the materials from Bering Sinkhole. These analyses proceed from the specifics of burial attributes such as the skeletal and artifactual materials, to the reconstruction of general social structure attributes as indicated by the accompanying ritual residues.

Because of the stratified nature of the burial data, a diachronic perspective is taken to compare one time period with another, thus providing a means of tracking the elaboration of mortuary practices through the central Texas Archaic periods. With each level of abstraction, the diachronic perspective provides relative comparisons between preceding and succeeding cultural systems. In the final instance, the reconstructions of the Archaic lifeways derived from mortuary data are compared and contrasted with those proposed from nonmortuary materials.

4. Field Techniques

Discovery and Exploration of Bering Sinkhole

Bering Sinkhole was initially located by the landowner and his ranch foreman. At the time of discovery, the entrance hole was partially obscured by low brush, and a dead tree protruded from the opening. When cleared of vegetation and loose rubble, the entrance was an elliptical hole 3.8 meters long and 2.1 meters wide in a nearly level limestone bench along the right bank of a small drainage (Figure 2). North and west of the entrance, the land rises gently, channeling surface runoff into the cavern. Deposits in the cavern came within 3 meters of the surface, or 2.7 meters from the ceiling at the rim of the entrance (Figure 2). With the exception of the tree protruding from the entrance, little vegetation grew within the cavern.

The unfilled portion of the cavern is an arched room approximately 4 meters wide at the south end under the entrance, narrowing to .5 meter wide at a point 10 meters north of the entrance (Figure 2). Maximum ceiling height varies from 2.7 meters near the entrance to 1 meter at a point 10 meters to the north. The chamber constricts even further to a shaft .3 meter wide and from .75 to 1.25 meters high for a minimum of 4.5 to 5 meters beyond the 10-meter mark. The horizontal shaft becomes impassable for humans at this point but continues for an undetermined distance.

At the time of discovery, entry into the cavern was possible only by climbing down the dead tree protruding from the entrance (Bering 1987). Without the tree, movement of people in and out of the cavern would have required the aid of a pole, ladder, or rope. Although the bedrock around the entrance to the sinkhole had been damaged by machine excavation prior to the archaeological investigations, there is no trace of intentional alteration of the entrance hole in prehistoric times.

Machine Excavation

Interest and curiosity about the size and extent of the cavern prompted the landowner to probe beneath the surface of the sinkhole using a track hoe (large backhoe) placed astride the opening. From this position, the hoe bucket scraped dirt from the cavern, dumping it in low piles around the east, south, and west periphery of the limestone bench. A hole approximately 2 meters wide by 4 meters long by 2 meters deep was excavated in this manner (Figure 2). Monitoring of this activity by the landowner, his family, and friends led to the recovery of numerous human and animal bones at varying depths in the fill. Included in the skeletal material was the complete cranium and a portion of the vertebral column of a wolf recovered at a depth of approximately 20 centimeters below the cavern surface and numerous human crania and postcranial fragments from approximately 1.25 meters to 2 meters below the cavern surface. When the skeletal material was recognized as human, the mechanical excavation ceased, and the landowner contacted archaeologists at the University of Texas at San Antonio (UTSA) and the University of Texas at Austin (UT-Austin). Dr. Joel Gunn of UTSA visited the site at the landowner's request and confirmed the recovery of prehistoric human skeletal remains.

Following a preliminary site visit by Solveig Turpin and Leland Bement, hand excavations were performed at various times throughout the period from June 1987 through March 1991.

Systematic Excavation

The excavation conducted by UT-Austin was intended to identify and salvage any pertinent information or materials uncovered by the mechanical explorations, to assess the potential for additional human as well as paleontological skeletal remains, and to determine the vertical and horizontal extent of the cavern. To these ends, the excavation procedures included the cleaning and documentation of the track hoe excavation, downward and lateral extension of the track hoe pit, and the collection of special samples for further analysis.

Excavation Techniques

A three-dimensional grid system tied to permanent horizontal and vertical datums was imposed on the site. All matrix was removed in arbitrary 10-centimeter-thick levels tied to a permanent datum and was water screened through one-fourth-inch and window mesh hardware cloth; the resultant fine-screen material was bagged and labeled according to provenience. Whenever possible, specimens were mapped in place prior to removal and labeled with special care taken to record strike and dip measurements and to stabilize fragile materials prior to extraction. This latter task proved quite formidable because of the highly fractured condition of the bone and the high moisture content of the deposits. To overcome these hardships, the bones were encased in spray foam insulation (see Bement 1985a). Once the bones were removed from the sinkhole and allowed to dry, many were treated with Gelva (acetone-cut polyvinyl acetate), a hardener and preservative.

As part of the documentation process, black-and-white and color photographs were taken of key in situ specimens and of the excavation procedures in general. Running water was supplied to the screening area by a hose from a well on the property, and electricity from the ranch house illuminated the dark recesses of the excavation units.

Initially, four test units were laid out to provide gross provenience references during the excavation. These units, a–d (Figure 2), were placed along the east side of the bottom of the track hoe pit where the cavern wall began to expand or bell out. Each unit was 1 meter long, following a north-south line, and approximately 70 centimeters wide. As excavation progressed, the units were widened to conform to the curvature of the cavern wall. The exposure of long bones also prompted the widening of units toward the center of the track hoe pit so that the entire specimen could be removed. Eleven additional units extended the excavation area to the west by 100 centimeters, north by 200 centimeters, and south by 50 centimeters (Figure 2).

Results of the Excavation

The hand excavation conducted by UT-Austin archaeologists removed approximately 18 cubic meters of deposits, containing identifiable human and nonhuman bone elements and artifacts of lithic, bone, shell, and antler. The quantity of matrix removed by the hand operation is slightly greater than the 16 cubic meters of deposits extracted by the track hoe. The well-provenienced samples from hand excavation provide the context needed to reconstruct the depositional sequence, morphological changes in the depositional cone surface, and the processes affecting the deposition of specimens.

The Application of Subsurface Interface Radar

In an attempt to determine the size of the subterranean vault, the nondestructive ground-probing technique of subsurface interface ra-

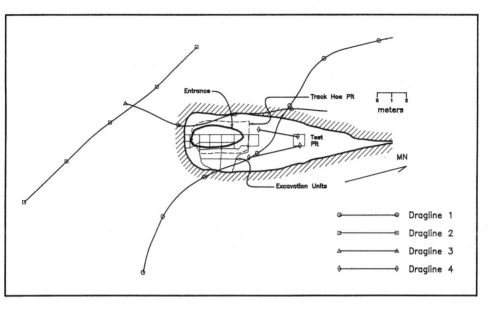

Figure 3. The location of subsurface interface radar transects and soundings at Bering Sinkhole.

dar (SIR) was applied before intensive excavation began in the immediate vicinity and within Bering Sinkhole. The presence of human skeletal remains precluded the use of destructive probing techniques, such as core drilling, for determining the vertical and horizontal extent of the deposits. The opportunity for SIR investigation was afforded when a Halliburton crew from Liberty, Texas, conducted SIR at a nearby dam site.

Five traverses and one stationary point were conducted (Figure 3). Three traverses were placed above ground; two more, on the surface within the sinkhole; and the stationary point was placed at the bottom of the excavation unit within the sinkhole deposits.

At the onset, it was expected that the surface paths would produce reflections of the horizontal extent of the sinkhole. In reality, the recordings fell short of expectations, partly as a result of moisture content of the sinkhole fill and the less-than-perfect path placement—a product of tree cover and highly uneven surfaces.

The three surface draglines intersected the long axis of the sinkhole fault line at different angles and produced varying results. Subsurface voids were found to extend along the long axis for a distance of approximately 10 meters to the south of the sinkhole opening. It was difficult to determine the size of the unconformities because of apparent high moisture levels in the limestone and fill.

In addition to the three surface draglines, short drags were performed on the surface of the deposits within the chamber (Figure 3).
Beginning at the northernmost point of sufficient size for the transceiver, the drags progressed from the center along either the west or
east sides for a distance of 5 meters to the edge of the excavation pits.
These short drags produced profiles that showed the extension of the
subsurface limestone benching north of opened pits, thus verifying
the dragline 1 profile. The dampness of the sinkhole deposits ob-
structed any attempts at deep soundings. As a final attempt to determine the maximum depth of the deposit, the transceiver was placed
on the floor of the excavation unit for a stationary reading. This reading was compared to those from the deposit surface drags for interpretation. The stationary profile suggests that the silty sinkhole deposits continue downward for an estimated 3 meters, at which time
penetration ceased. No bottom was identified.

The application of the nondestructive subsurface investigative technique of subsurface interfacing radar indicates that Bering Sinkhole
continues to the south an additional 10 meters and that the main
chamber is approximately 3 meters deeper than the 2.5-meter-deep
track hoe pit.

Results of Additional Hand Units

To check the accuracy of the SIR readings, excavation units were
placed 1.5 meters north of the track hoe pit where dragline 1 crossed
the chamber. This unit, Unit H, confirmed the continuation of the
crevice between the limestone benches and the belling out of the
chamber below the benches. Units M, N, and O were placed along
the south end of the track hoe pit to determine if the chamber continues southward as indicated by draglines 2 and 3. These units revealed
that a continuous limestone wall extends to the bottom of the deposits. Much of this limestone is covered in flowstone. A small shaft,
50 centimeters in diameter, in the west side of Unit M is full of limestone blocks and may be the shaft registered by the SIR that continues
southward. The main chamber, however, does not continue to the
south at the levels containing the burials.

The downward extension of the excavation units plumbed an additional 2.5 meters before hitting impenetrable flowstone and large
limestone boulders. I interpret the undulating limestone and flowstone as the floor of the cavern. We were unable to penetrate the
substrate beyond approximately 15 centimeters with the aid of rock
hammers and picks. The limestone became progressively harder, and
it appeared that we were removing decomposing limestone bedrock

at this point. Until a larger area of the cavern is opened to this level, it is impossible to ascertain if the bedrock floor of the cavern has been reached.

A 1-by-1-meter test pit was also placed 3 meters north of Unit H in an attempt to ascertain the extent of the limestone benching. The northern two-thirds of this unit hit solid limestone at 30 centimeters below the surface. The southern one-third uncovered the beginning of the cleft that continues downward into the main cavern. The limestone bench at this point is 75 centimeters thick. Below the bench, the chamber appears to open or bell out in all directions. The small size of the test pit, however, precludes determining the extent of the expansion in this area.

5. Depositional Reconstruction and Dating

The excavation deposits in Bering Sinkhole are composed of four distinct depositional units, here numbered from top to bottom (Figure 4). The uppermost unit, Unit I, is a black clay loam with limestone cobbles and pebbles that extends from the interior sinkhole surface to an approximate depth of 2.3 meters. Five radiocarbon dates (Table 2) were obtained from this deposit: 990 ± 140 (Tx-6525) and 1085 ± 60 (Pitt 0073) at 190 centimeters below the sinkhole deposit surface; 2130 ±80 (Tx-6921) at 220 centimeters below the surface; and 2560 ± 80 (Tx-5877) and 2610 ± 280 (Tx-6167) at 240 centimeters below the surface.

The first two dates from Unit I were from charcoal from an unknown source recovered halfway through the upper deposit; the third date was from charcoal associated with the uppermost cremation from the site; and the remaining two dates from Unit I were from a cremation immediately above the Unit I/II contact. The overlap in the ranges after calibration of the latter two dates suggests that both samples originated from a single cremation that distributed charcoal as it dispersed down the debris cone surface. If both samples are from the same cremation, the slope of the cone surface at the time of deposition was approximately 33 percent (9 degrees 5 minutes).

Unit II is approximately 80 centimeters thick and consists of a matrix of dark brown clay loam enveloping limestone cobbles and pebbles. A single uncalibrated date of 3420 ± 100 B.P. (Tx-6135) was obtained from charcoal collected from 25 centimeters below the Unit I/II contact. The origin of this charcoal is uncertain, although the recovery of burned bone at the same level suggests that it too is from a cremation. This sample produces a range of 3829 to 3569 B.P. after calibration. The in situ plotting of bones and artifacts reveals that the Unit II surface was a half cone, with slopes ranging from 50 percent (26 degrees 34 minutes) along the N–S axis to 25 percent (14 degrees 2 minutes) along the E–W axis of the cavern.

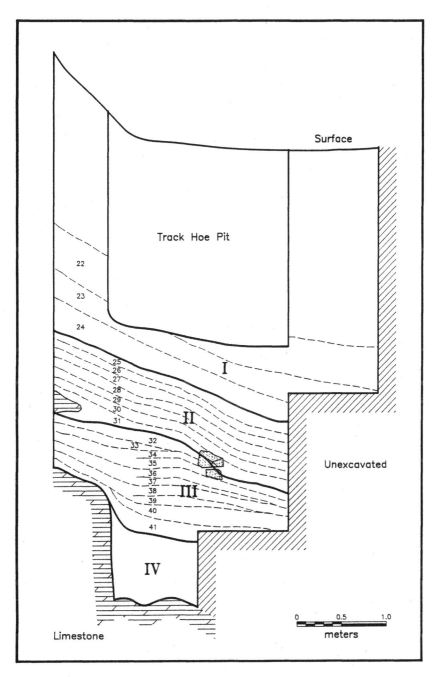

Figure 4. This profile along the west wall of the excavation units illustrates the relationship of analysis levels to the four major depositional levels, Units I–IV.

Table 2. *Radiocarbon Dates from Bering Sinkhole (expressed in radiocarbon years B.P., range of calibrated calendrical years B.P., and associated provenience)*

Lab No.	Date	Calibrated Range B.P. [a]	Level	Unit
Tx-6525	990 ± 140	1060–740	19	I
Pitt 0073	1085 ± 60	1060–939	19	I
Tx-6921	2130 ± 80	2303–2021	22	I
Tx-5877	2560 ± 80	2758–2498	24	I
Tx-6167	2610 ± 280	3009–2349	24	I
Tx-6135	3420 ± 100	3829–3569	26	II
Tx-6282	5840 ± 190	6889–6439	37	III
Tx-6831	6660 ± 110	7589–7429	40	III
Tx-6526	6860 ± 170	7907–7518	40	III

[a] Calibrated one-sigma range after Stuiver and Pearson 1986.

Unit III is 1.2 meters thick and consists of a reddish brown clay with limestone cobbles and pebbles. The slope of the Unit II/III contact is 10 percent (5 degrees 43 minutes) along the N–S axis. Three uncalibrated radiocarbon dates of 5840 ± 190 B.P. (Tx-6282), 6660 ± 110 (Tx-6831), and 6860 ± 170 B.P. (Tx-6526) were obtained from large pieces of charcoal of unknown source recovered at a depth of 60 centimeters, 100 centimeters, and 110 centimeters below the Unit II/III contact, respectively. These dates range 6889–6439 B.P., 7589–7429 B.P., and 7907–7518 B.P., respectively, after calibration.

Unit IV consists of friable limestone spalls partially cemented in tan clay flowstone. Although the bottom of the cavern has not been reached, this lowest excavated unit produced no cultural or datable organic material.

In summary, the 5.25 meters of cavern fill below the depositional surface represent over 7,000 years of use of the sinkhole as an inaccessible mortuary site. The Unit IV deposits are devoid of human remains and possibly date to the late Pleistocene. Unit III is between 7,600 and 5,100 years old. Unit II deposits range from 5,100 to 3,100 years in age, and the uppermost deposits, Unit I, date from 3,100 years ago to the present.

Using the midpoints of the calibrated radiocarbon dates and the vertical positioning of the samples, it was possible to estimate the overall accumulation rates of each unit. Unit I deposits between level 19 and level 22 accumulated at a rate of .026 centimeters per year. From level 22 to the contact with Unit II in level 25, a rate of .032 cm/yr was

Table 3. *Estimated Duration in Calendrical Years*
B.P. of Each Analysis Level

	Level	Age Range (Cal. yrs. B.P.)
Unit I	19	790–1175
	20	1175–1560
	21	1560–1945
	22	1945–2330
	23	2330–2715
	24	2715–3100
Unit II	25	3100–3400
	26	3400–3700
	27	3700–3980
	28	3980–4260
	29	4260–4540
	30	4540–4820
	31	4820–5100
Unit III	32	5100–5380
	33	5380–5660
	34	5660–5940
	35	5940–6220
	36	6220–6500
	37	6500–6780
	38	6780–7050
	39	7050–7320
	40	7320–7590
	41	7590–7760
Unit IV	42	Pleistocene?

obtained. The upper three levels of Unit II accumulated at a rate of
.032 cm/yr, and from level 26 through level 37, the rate is estimated
at .036 cm/yr. Levels 37, 38, 39, and 40 accrued at a rate of .037 cm/yr,
and level 41 accumulated at a slightly accelerated rate of .058 cm/yr.
These rates and associated radiocarbon dates place the boundaries of
the major units at pre-7760 B.P. for the Unit IV/III contact, 5100 B.P.
for the Unit III/II contact, and 3100 B.P. for the Unit II/I contact.

The upper levels of Unit I accumulated at an accelerated rate of .19
cm/yr due to the constriction of the sinkhole walls. The relationship
between cavern morphology and deposition of the upper levels of
Unit I are problematic. However, the similarity in cavern shape for
the pre-1,000-year-old levels allows the estimation of ages for each
of the pre-1,000-year-old 10 centimeter excavation levels (Table 3).

Correlation of Deposits

The eleven excavation units that compose the main excavation block were excavated in arbitrary 10-centimeter levels. Due to the apparent steep slope of the depositional cone, the various levels of each unit do not correspond with the same level number in a neighboring unit as would be the case if all deposition was horizontally level. Thus, correlating the various levels of the different units was crucial to the sorting of the cultural material and determining the number of burial levels in the sinkhole. The following section presents the methods employed to correlate the various units and levels.

Debris Cone Development

The depositional sequence in the sinkhole varied in relationship to proximity to the cavern wall and location on the aggrading debris cone. The excavations, to date, indicate the cavern extends to the north for an undetermined distance believed to be some tens of meters. The east wall is within 3 meters of the center of the entrance, and the south wall is less than 50 centimeters away. It is believed that the west wall is similarly less than 3 meters from the center directly under the opening. Thus, as the debris cone under the surface opening aggraded, the east, west, and south slopes contacted the cavern walls, causing the quick buildup of deposits in these areas, while the northern slope remained comparatively open and unobstructed and was characterized by thinner deposits.

The debris cone originated on a travertine-coated cavern floor or on the tops of very large breakdown blocks. This floor was level under the opening and then sloped to the north. The Unit IV deposits mirrored the floor morphology: level in the center and sloping to the north along the northern edge of the excavation block.

The debris cone aggraded quickly during Unit III deposition as large limestone blocks accumulated. These blocks, reaching sizes of 10-by-20-by-40 centimeters, consisted of roof fall and intrusive material probably thrown on top of burials. The aggradation of sediments around the blocks was sufficient to maintain a near-level floor, which is partly attributable to the nearness of the three cavern walls that served to deflect deposits back toward the center. However, the north-facing deposits continued to slope in that direction.

At the beginning of Unit II deposition, heightened intrusion of limestone rubble and blocks, concomitant with the expansion of the cavern area due to the outward curve of the walls, led to the disproportionate buildup of the cone compared to the sediment around it.

Thus, the cone increased in size at a faster rate than the surrounding area, resulting in steeply sloping surfaces. The cavern walls continued to redirect sediments, thus maintaining a surface with less slope than that to the north. By the end of Unit II deposition, the north-facing surface had a slope of 50 percent (26 degrees 34 minutes) compared to a 25 percent (14 degrees 2 minutes) slope toward the east wall. At this point, over 2 meters of sediment and rubble had collected under the opening, and the apex of the debris cone was at the constriction separating the bottom chamber from the upper chamber of the cavern.

Between 20 and 30 centimeters of Unit I deposits were required to fill the eastern void of the lower chamber, after which time all material was channeled down the north surface of the cone. The constriction of the cavern walls increased the rate at which the deposits accrued under the opening. By the time the constricted portion under the opening was filled, the sinkhole was no longer used as a mortuary site. Deposition continued, but limestone rubble was no longer a component. Two meters of fine sediments filled the constricted area and the lower portions of the upper chamber.

The differential cone morphology has significant implications for correlating the levels of the various excavation units. For the most part, the deposits for a given temporal unit, say 250 years, were differentially distributed in the lower chamber in relation to the east, west, and south cavern walls, debris cone, and north slope. If buildup on the cone was 10 centimeters for a 250-year period, the buildup on the steep north slope would be less than 10 centimeters and that along the close walls would be more than 10 centimeters. With the constriction of the walls during Unit I deposition, the area between the cone apex and the south wall would increase almost four times faster than that along the north slope.

In order to define and verify changes in depositional relationships, all long bones, artifacts, and large tabular limestone blocks were mapped in place, and strike and dip measurements were taken. In this fashion, the slope of the depositional surface could be projected from excavation unit to unit. An example of how this worked in defining the depositional pattern of the Unit I deposits is provided here.

Unit k consists of the remnant of the deposition cone directly under the opening and against the south wall. It provided the only intact upper cone area, since the rest of the cone in these levels was removed by track hoe excavation. The uppermost skeletal remains in this unit occurred at 110 to 120 centimeters below the surface and consisted of a cremation intermixed with nonburned human remains. Also in this uppermost level were pockets of bone beads, some with beads lying end to end as if on a string. Pockets contained up to 80 beads as if the string of beads had been in a pouch.

The nonburned and partially burned human remains were deposited on what must have been a very narrow, steep-sided cone apex. The vertical distribution of burned elements of a single cremation provided evidence of the depositional history of this area. The fragments from a single burned skull were recovered from a 50-centimeter-square area. The vertical distribution of the pieces was a surprising 30 centimeters. The implication here is that the cone was very steep and that the horizontal size of Unit k (50-by-50) actually encompassed what in level depositional situations would include three 10-centimeter levels. In essence, the deposits appeared to have been turned on edge and were aggrading in a horizontal fashion away from the south wall. Confirmation of the extremely steep cone surface came from the fact that no pieces of this cremation were found at similar elevations in the excavation units north of the track hoe pit. Thus, the cone surface dropped in elevation faster than it progressed horizontally.

A less complicated surface was identified by a cache of large bifaces (see chapter 7). The main concentration of bifaces was found in an area 50 centimeters north-south by 60 centimeters east-west (Bement 1991). Two outliers were located 50 centimeters north and 70 centimeters northeast of the main group. The clustering of the specimens suggests that the cache entered the sinkhole in a bag or pouch or possibly wrapped and placed with a corpse. The vertical distribution of the bifaces defines the surface of a quadrant of the cone, with the highest point in Unit e—nearest the vertical entrance of the sinkhole—sloping downward to the north and northeast. The slope of the cone to the north was defined by the vertical displacement of 10 centimeters for every 20 centimeters of horizontal movement defining a 50 percent slope (26 degrees 34 minutes). A gradient along a vector 90 degrees east of north consisted of only a 5-centimeter drop for every 20 centimeters of horizontal displacement or 25 percent slope (14 degrees 2 minutes).

In this fashion, the main burial units and depositional surfaces were correlated between excavation units and formed the basis for the correlation of the various levels into analytical units. A total of forty-one analytical units or levels was defined from the surface in the cavern to the bottom of the Unit III deposits.

6. Faunal Analysis

Contained within the Bering Sinkhole deposits were the partial remains of numerous animals. These remains were segregated into mammalian and molluscan categories for analysis. The identification of the mammalian fauna and the subsequent analysis allows us to reconstruct the succession of animal communities through time in this area of the Edwards Plateau. The molluscan analysis was performed by Raymond W. Neck, a biologist with the Texas Parks and Wildlife Department, Austin (Neck 1991). His analysis was limited to the snails contained in twelve samples of fine-screen matrix corresponding to select levels of the stratigraphic column. The mammalian and molluscan analyses were structured to provide paleoenvironmental data where possible. The nonmammalian and nonmolluscan faunal remains have not been analyzed except in the case of a turtle carapace artifact.

Mammalian Fauna

The following material describes and analyzes the nonhuman mammalian remains recovered from the hand excavation of Holocene deposits in Bering Sinkhole. Dentition and cranial elements were used in the identification process. A total of 26 genera were identified (Table 4). An accounting of each taxon is presented in the Appendix. The mammalian remains are relevant to several key paleontological and archaeological issues on the Edwards Plateau region of Texas.

Taphonomy of Mammalian Fauna

Faunal remains are deposited in the caves and caverns of the Edwards Plateau through various processes. Among these processes or agents are water transport of already dead and decomposed animals; capture and transport by birds and animals of prey; entrapment of living ani-

Table 4 *Taxa of Mammals from Bering Sinkhole*

Class Mammalia
  Order Marsupialia
    Family Didelphiidae
      Didelphis virginiana   Opossum
  Order Xenarthra
    Family Dasypodidae
      Dasypus novemcinctus   Armadillo
  Order Lagomorpha
    Family Leporidae
      Lepus californicus   Black-tailed jackrabbit
      Sylvilagus sp.   Cottontail rabbit
      Sylvilagus floridanus   Eastern cottontail
      Sylvilagus audubonii   Audubon's cottontail
  Order Rodentia
    Family Sciuridae
      Spermophilus mexicanus   Mexican ground squirrel
    Family Geomyidae
      Thomomys bottae   Botta's pocket gopher
      Geomys bursarius   Plains pocket gopher
      Pappogeomys castanops   Yellow-faced pocket gopher
    Family Heteromyidae
      Perognathus sp.   Pocket mouse
    Family Cricetidae
      Microtus sp.   Vole
      Peromyscus sp.   White-footed mouse
      Onychomys leucogaster   Grasshopper mouse
      Neotoma sp.   Woodrat
      Sigmodon hispidus   Hispid cotton rat
  Order Insectivora
      Notiosorex crawfordi   Desert shrew
  Order Carnivora
    Family Mustelidae
      Mustela frenata   Long-tailed weasel
      Conepatus mesoleucus   Hog-nosed skunk
      Taxidea taxus   Badger
    Family Canidae
      Canis familiaris   Domestic dog
      Canis latrans   Coyote
      Canis lupus   Gray wolf
    Family Procyonidae
      Procyon lotor   Raccoon
    Family Ursidae
      Ursus americanus   Black bear
  Order Artiodactyla
    Family Cervidae
      Odocoileus virginianus   White-tailed deer
    Family Bovidae
      Bison bison   Bison

mals in a deadfall trap; and the natural death of animals in a den. Regardless of the agent responsible for the introduction of an animal to the cavern, the corpse is subjected to destructive forces that disarticulate and distribute the skeletal remains over the surface of the cavern deposits. These forces include rodent gnawing, water action, roof spall crushing, and to a limited degree, root scarring.

The mammalian remains entered the sinkhole through the vertical shaft entrance. Dalquest, Roth, and Judd (1969) attribute the numerous and varied microfaunal remains in Schulze Cave, in neighboring Edwards County, to owls, based on the similarity of fracture patterns in the cave fauna with those observed in recent owl pellets. The recovery of a single consolidated owl pellet in the uppermost level of Bering Sinkhole indicates this mode of transport is at least partially responsible for the small fauna at this site.

Other animals are believed to have fallen into or entered the cavern and been unable to escape. Animals trapped in this fashion include wolves, coyotes, and possibly domestic dogs. Many of the rodents probably fell into the cavern in the same fashion as the larger mammals. The extreme gnawing observed on much of the human and larger animal remains suggests that some of the small rodents survived the fall and resorted to eating bone before dying of probable starvation.

The recovery of single elements of taxa such as the isolated bison hooves in levels 10 and 11 and possibly the bear mandible in level 23 are probably the result of the water transport of materials around and upslope of the sinkhole opening. The fact the teeth were still in the bear mandible suggests this specimen was close to the opening and not subject to long distance transport, had not been on the surface for long before entering the sinkhole, or had been deliberately placed in the sinkhole as a burial offering. Support of the last possibility is found in the correlation of this material with human burials. A similar case is seen in the distribution of deer antler.

The high incidence of shed antler, antlered skulls, and burned antler during post-5000 B.P. times suggests that human agents are responsible for their inclusion in the sinkhole. The inclusion of antlers with prehistoric human burials is well documented from isolated burials on the Edwards Plateau (Bement 1987) and mortuary sites in the coastal plain (Lukowski 1988; Taylor and Highley n.d.).

Distribution of Taxa by Level

The distribution of identified fauna by level provides a successional history of the animals inhabiting the area in the vicinity of Bering

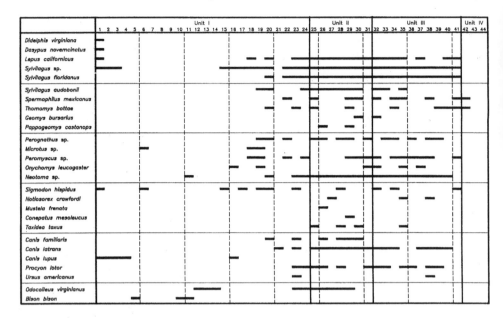

Figure 5. The vertical distribution of mammalian fauna in Bering Sinkhole.

Sinkhole during the Holocene between 8000 B.P. and the present (Figure 5). *Lepus californicus, S. floridanus, Neotoma* sp., *Canis latrans*, and *Procyon lotor* are consistently represented throughout the 8,000-year span. All other taxa, including *Spermophilus mexicanus, Microtus* sp., *Sigmodon hispidus, Onychomys leucogaster*, and *Taxidea taxus*, are either sporadically represented or have single occurrences. Limited representations, particularly by the carnivores *Ursus americanus, Conepatus mesoleucus, Mustela frenata*, and *Canis lupus*, are not reliable indicators of the succession of fauna in the area, although their presence may be significant in broad regional studies.

Black bears were found in only two, widely separated levels and so their presence is difficult to interpret in terms of possible changes in the faunal assemblage. The *Ursus americanus* remains were found in levels containing human burials, suggesting that humans are responsible for their inclusion in the sinkhole.

Sixteen of the 26 taxa were represented in the Unit III deposits and continue into Unit II. Three taxa, *Pappogeomys castanops, Conepatus mesoleucus*, and *Mustela frenata*, are distributed only in the Unit II deposits, and of the Unit III taxa, *Notiosorex crawfordi, Geomys bursarius*, and *Taxidea taxus* are last represented in Unit II. The only taxon to first appear in Unit II and continue into Unit I is *Canis familiaris*. Five taxa,

Bison bison, Microtus sp., *Canis lupus, Didelphis virginiana,* and *Dasypus novemcinctus,* joined the assemblage in the Unit I deposits.

Paleoenvironmental Reconstruction

Observed changes in plant communities through time, as represented in the pollen record, suggest that the environment on the Edwards Plateau and neighboring regions has varied during the Quaternary. A model of these changes has been outlined for the late
Quaternary period, roughly spanning 33,500 B.P. to the present. This
time frame includes the Wisconsin Interpluvial (33,500–22,500 B.P.),
Wisconsin Fullglacial (22,500–14,000 B.P.), Lateglacial (14,000–10,000
B.P.), and Postglacial (10,000–0 B.P.) (Bryant and Shafer 1977). Additional information on the changing environmental conditions has
been gained through the study of faunal remains from the caves of
the Edwards Plateau (Toomey 1990; Lundelius 1967).

During the Wisconsin Interpluvial, the environment of west Texas
was a scrub grassland with widely scattered trees and a cool and
moist climate. Although no evidence from central Texas is directly
applicable to this time period, extrapolations from similar areas to
the north and east suggest that central Texas was probably a grassland with herbaceous plants and a few scattered conifers (Bryant and
Shafer 1977).

During the Wisconsin Fullglacial (22,500–14,000 B.P.), conifers and
deciduous trees expanded their ranges, reducing the grasslands of
central Texas. Pollen data from west and central Texas show a rapid
increase in the percentages of spruce and pine pollen (Bryant and
Shafer 1977:8), as well as pollen from basswood, maple, poplar, and
alder. Specifically from central Texas, pine and oak pollen percentages are low during the Fullglacial period. Support for a forested
central Texas during the Fullglacial is provided by faunal species such
as the giant beaver (*Castoroides* sp.), the long-nosed peccary (*Mylohyus*
sp.), the mastodon (*Mammut* sp.), and the tapir (*Tapirus* sp.) (Graham
1976; Slaughter 1963). The faunal record also indicates the climate was
cooler and wetter during the Fullglacial than it was during the Interpluvial. Such species as the masked shrew (*Sorex cinereus*) and the bog
lemming (*Synaptomys cooperi*), which disappear early in the Postglacial, are found today in northern areas of North America where the
climate is colder and wetter (Lundelius 1967, 1974, 1986). The faunal
remains agree with the pollen evidence for this period.

The Lateglacial period (14,000–10,000 B.P.) in central Texas reduced
woodlands and parklands and increased scrub grasslands compared

to the Fullglacial period. This is supported by pollen records from the Llano Estacado and central Texas (Hafsten 1961; Oldfield and Schoenwetter 1975; Bryant 1977). Certain tree species, including willow, birch, spruce, basswood, alder, tupelo, and ash, were gone from central Texas by the end of the Lateglacial period (Bryant and Shafer 1977). This is also the period of extinction for many of the large mammals, including the Jeffersonian mammoth (*Mammuthus jeffersonii*), American mastodon (*Mammut americanum*), saber-toothed cat (*Smilodon floridanus*), dire wolf (*Canis dirus*), and Harlan's ground sloth (*Glossotherium harlani*) (Lundelius 1986; Martin 1984). Certain smaller extant species left the central Texas region and today are found to the north and east in cooler, wetter climates or have limited central Texas distributions in the canyons along the Balcones Escarpment. Among these species are the masked shrew (*Sorex cinereus*), short-tailed shrew (*Blarina* sp.), ermine (*Mustela erminea*), southern bog lemming (*Synaptomys cooperi*), meadow vole (*Microtus pennsylvanicus*), eastern chipmunk (*Tamais striatus*), and the pine vole (*Pitymys pinetorum*) (Lundelius 1986; Toomey 1990). The Lateglacial period had a warmer and drier environment than the preceding Fullglacial.

A continuation in the trend toward aridity and warmer climates is postulated for the Postglacial period (10,000 B.P. to the present). This is supported by pollen analysis of peat bogs in central Texas (Bryant 1977). Pollen analysis indicates a further reduction in the percentage of tree pollen and a corresponding increase in the percentages of herb and grass pollen. A significant exception to the decrease in tree pollen is an increase in the percentage of oak (*Quercus* sp.) pollen. During the Altithermal (7000–4500 B.P.) (Antevs 1955), the central Texas pollen data indicates the continuation of the trend toward more xeric vegetation and the inference for a warmer and drier climate (Bryant and Shafer 1977:18). In addition, the pollen record indicates that the post oak savanna seen in central Texas today was more or less established by 3000 B.P. The faunal record shows greater variation in the climate during the Postglacial period.

Dillehay (1974), in studying the distribution of bison remains in prehistoric sites, identifies various presence and absence periods for central Texas, each attributed to differing climatic conditions. His Presence Period I (12,000–7000 B.P.) includes a portion of the Lateglacial period and indicates bison, in this case *Bison antiquus* and later *Bison occidentalis* were in central Texas. From 7000 B.P. to 4500 B.P., the period of the Altithermal, bison were no longer on the southern Plains in Texas (Dillehay 1974:181). Bison, this time in the modern form of *Bison bison*, appear in archaeological sites during Presence Period II (4500–1500 B.P.) and then are absent during Absence Period

II (1500–400 B.P.) only to reappear after 400 B.P. Bison presence periods are equated with mesic intervals in the otherwise trend to increased xeric conditions. The post-2000 B.P. time frame is not considered in the Bryant and Shafer (1977) model because of the apparent paucity of preserved pollen for this period in Texas (Bryant and Shafer 1977).

Hulbert (1984) proposes a climatic model using the eastward advance and westward retreat of the range of *Sylvilagus audubonii* (desert cottontail) across the Edwards Plateau. The basic premise of this model is that the presence of the arid-adapted desert cottontail indicates increased xeric conditions, and the absence signifies mesic conditions beyond that tolerated by the desert rabbit. In this model, the period from 9000 B.P. to 5000 B.P. was more mesic than today; from 5000 B.P. to 3000 B.P. was more xeric; and from 3000 B.P. to 400 B.P. was comparable to the modern, more xeric conditions (Hulbert 1984: 203). Accompanying the desert cottontail is an increase in short grasses over tall grasses; and vice versa during the absence of this rabbit.

Certain taxa of mammals entered the central Texas area during the Postglacial. These include the nine-banded armadillo (*Dasypus novemcinctus*) and collared peccary (*Tayassu tajacu*) that entered the region within the last 300 years. Other species, including the rock squirrel (*Spermophilus variegatus*) and ringtail (*Bassariscus astutes*), entered the region during the Holocene, but the exact time has not been determined (Lundelius 1986:45). The paleoenvironment, particularly the Holocene reconstruction, is considered further in chapter 9.

Hulbert's (1984) environmental reconstruction of the Holocene of western Texas is based on the presence or absence of certain leporid taxa, specifically the waxing and waning of the distributions of the desert cottontail and Florida cottontail. The distribution of the desert cottontail and Florida cottontail is tied to the availability of water and is related to the mean annual rainfall. Thus, these rabbit species are considered gross indicators of paleoprecipitation.

The eastern boundary of the desert cottontail (*Sylvilagus audubonii*) in Texas now approximates the eastern edge of the Edwards Plateau (Balcones Escarpment). A western movement of this boundary would indicate higher precipitation rates for the plateau. In order to test Hulbert's proposition and to see its effect on the central Edwards Plateau, the leporid materials from the dated stratigraphic deposits of Bering Sinkhole (41KR241) were identified to species using the discriminant criteria presented by Hulbert (1984) and plotted according to their vertical or stratigraphic provenience (Figure 5). In an attempt to substantiate the identification of *S. audubonii* in the sinkhole deposits, the bullae from all *Sylvilagus* and *Lepus* were compared with specimens from the recent collections at the Texas Archeological Research Laboratory (TARL) and the Texas Memorial Museum Vertebrate Paleontology Laboratory (TMM-VP). A total of 25 bullae from the sinkhole were identified as *S. floridanus*, 13 as *Lepus*, and 2 as *S. audubonii*. The small number of definitely identified *S. audubonii* bullae is attributed to the relative fragility of this element in *S. audubonii* as compared to either *Lepus* or *S. floridanus*. The two *S. audubonii* bullae are from levels containing maxillae attributed to *S. audubonii* by Hulbert's formula and thus support the identification of this rabbit in Bering Sinkhole fauna.

The earliest faunal remains in the sinkhole date to around 8000 B.P. From 8000 to 5800, the inventory includes both jackrabbit (*Lepus californicus*) and Florida cottontail (*Sylvilagus floridanus*). The desert cottontail (*S. audubonii*) first appears in the 5,800-year-old deposits. The desert cottontail occurs sporadically until approximately 4,300 years ago (age estimated from derived deposition rates in these lower levels), after which it occurs continuously up to 2,700 years ago, when definitely identifiable remains of the desert cottontail disappear for approximately 1,000 years. The rabbit remains in the post-1,000-year-old deposits could not be identified to species.

Following the assumptions used by Hulbert, the sinkhole material suggests that before 5,800 years ago (8000–5800 B.P.) mean annual precipitation was higher than today; 5800–4300 B.P. saw a trend to relatively less precipitation, leveling out between 4,300 and 2,700 years ago; 2,700–1,000 years ago precipitation increased; and after 1,000 years ago precipitation decreased and may have approximated the modern level. Wherever identifiable specimens were recovered, *S. floridanus* is present, indicating that the drier periods never reached the point of driving out the Florida rabbit. Today, both species are found throughout the southern Edwards Plateau (Davis 1978).

Gophers provide another indicator of past environments. Their ranges are tied less to temperature and rainfall than to soil depth. As the soil depth diminishes, the gopher species is replaced by one adapted to shallower and more rocky soils. The limited gopher materials recovered from the sinkhole indicate that the *Thomomys* and *Geomys* were sympatric in the vicinity of the sinkhole until the Unit II level 30, at which time *Geomys* was replaced by *Pappogeomys* (Figure 5). *Pappogeomys* was apparently no longer in the area after Unit II level 26. *Thomomys* remained in the area until Unit I level 19, which is dated at approximately 1,000 years ago. The eventual loss of all gophers by 1,000 years ago is tied to the reduction in soil depth across the plateau. This follows a general pattern observed at Schulze Cave in Edwards County (Dalquest, Roth, and Judd 1969) and at Halls Cave in Kerr County (Toomey 1990).

The few remains of *Microtus* sp. only appear in the sinkhole deposits in post-1000 B.P. levels, suggesting the limited expansion of favorable conditions from a nearby refugium of this species (Lundelius 1967).

Culturally Significant Fauna

Analysis of the Bering Sinkhole materials has identified fauna with a cultural reason for inclusion in the assemblage. Included in this category are turtle, rabbit, turkey, freshwater mussels, marine shellfish, and dogs. In addition, artifacts of deer, rabbit, and badger bone have distributions that overlap the nonartifact occurrence of these animals or are present in strata devoid of nonartifact elements. Rabbit and turkey are represented by bone beads; and deer, by one awl, one needle, and numerous antlers. A single bear claw may have cultural relevance as might a bear mandible recovered at the Unit I/II contact. The bones of dogs (*Canis familiaris*) may result from hapless activity or may have been intentionally placed in the sinkhole upon death.

Some of these materials rely on human agents for placement in the sinkhole. The marine shell is over 400 kilometers from its nearest possible source. A closer source is available for the freshwater mussels that include species known to occur in the Guadalupe and Llano rivers (Neck 1991). The nearest permanent water source with the potential for these materials is 16 kilometers north, along the Johnson Fork of the Llano River in Kimble County. Here, three large springs supply the perennial Johnson Fork. Similar springs flow 32 kilometers southeast of Bering Sinkhole along the Guadalupe River. A water source is likewise needed for the pond slider turtle carapace. The same potential suppliers of the mussel shell could have provided the pond slider turtle. The remaining fauna, turkey, deer, and badger, are common on the Edwards Plateau and could have been procured in the nearby drainages.

Both occurrences of bear are in strata containing human remains. The fact that one is a claw, and the other is a mandible half with teeth, elements often culturally important, suggests that cultural intervention cannot be ruled out.

Dog Remains and Other Texas Canids

Dog remains were recovered from Bering Sinkhole deposits dating to the Clear Fork Phase (5000–4000 B.P.), Round Rock Phase (4200–2600

B.P.), San Marcos Phase (2800–1800 B.P.), and Twin Sisters Phase (2000–700 B.P.). The presence of *C. familiaris* in the Bering Sinkhole deposits is attributed to one of two processes. First is the possibility that free-ranging dogs either fell into the sinkhole or jumped in much the same manner as the coyotes. The second possibility is that the dogs were placed in the sinkhole as burials or included with human burials. A strong correlation exists between the distribution of dog remains, deer antlers, bone beads, human cremations, and human skeletal remains. The recovery of *C. familiaris* postcranial remains indicates the entire animal was buried. While this correlation suggests the dogs were intentionally placed in the sinkhole, their presence may be the result of increased dog activity associated with more human activity levels within the drainages about the sinkhole during this time, thus allowing for an increased chance (probability) for inadvertent entrapment in the sinkhole.

A similar situation is found at the Schulze Cave sinkhole in neighboring Edwards County, where the remains of domestic dog were found in the 5,000-to-3,800-year-old deposits that also contained human burials (Dalquest, Roth, and Judd 1969). Again, it cannot be determined if the dogs were intentionally placed in the sinkhole.

The domestic dog has been identified at prehistoric sites across the state, although little study of their presence and morphology has been reported (Table 5). With the exception of the Bering dogs, all comparative materials are from site deposits dating to the Late Prehistoric or transitional Late Archaic/Late Prehistoric periods (after A.D. 600), and at least half are from horticultural groups. For purposes of comparison, the dog material from Kincaid Shelter, Winterbauer midden, and 41KF7 are presented. This is not a comprehensive or exhaustive comparison of Texas dogs. These sites have been chosen because they have animals identified as domestic dogs, and they contain the same cranial elements and dentitions that were recovered from Bering Sinkhole.

The most complete dog material considered in this analysis is from the Winterbauer site (41WO6), a Caddoan midden site in northeast Texas. A minimum of 14 dogs represented by cranial and postcranial remains were removed from the southern half of a large midden at this site (Jackson 1930). The MNI is set by the number of right mandibles, 1 loose right mandibular M1, and a left mandible fragment with an M1 with wear in excess of all right mandibular teeth. Eight left mandibles are also in the collection along with 5 crania with at least partial maxilla. Additional cranial and postcranial elements are present in the collection housed at the TMM Vertebrate Paleontology Laboratory.

Table 5 *Dogs from Archaeological Sites*

Site	County	Number of Dogs	Time Period	Provenience	Reference
Kincaid	Uvalde	4	Late Prehistoric	Zone 6	Collins (1990)
Winterbauer	Wood	14	Caddoan	Midden	TARL files
Gossett Bottoms	Kaufman	1	Caddoan	Midden	Story (1965)
Levi Fox	Williamson	1	Unknown	Midden	Prewitt (1982)
Britton	McLennan	3–4	Approx. 2000 B.P.	Feature 47	Story and Shafer (1965)
41AU36	Austin	1	Terminal Archaic	Zone 4	Hall (1981)
Unrecorded	Williamson	1	Unknown	Midden	Weir (1976)
Unrecorded	Travis	1	Unknown	Midden	Weir (1976)
Hinds Cave	Val Verde	unknown	Unknown	Unknown	Lord (1984:100)
Lacy Site	Henderson	1	Unknown	Pit	Story (1965)
Miller Site	Delta	1	Unknown	Pit	Johnson (1962)
Schulze Cave	Edwards	2	3800–5000 B.P.	Level B	Dalquest, Roth, and Judd (1969)

All dogs from the Winterbauer site are smaller than a coyote (Table 6), and cranial length measurements (nasal-occipital) fall within the small Indian dog range reported by Colton (1970:155). Tooth eruption and wear patterns indicate that individuals ranging in age from juvenile to senile are present. Incisor wear patterns indicate that prognathic and nonprognathic individuals are represented (one each). Unfortunately, the sample is too fragmentary to determine occlusal patterns of all specimens.

At 41KF7, a Caddoan midden in Kaufman County, a single dog specimen was represented by cranial and postcranial elements (Story 1965). The left palate including the right premaxillary to the left M2 and corresponding left mandible (C-M2) are from a small dog. The maxilla is missing the P1, although the mandibular P1 is present. Tooth row length indicates this dog was as short nosed as the Bering (392) sample. In addition to brachycephaly, the incisor wear patterns of the Kaufman specimen indicate that the lower jaw jutted prognathically beyond that of the maxilla.

A reexamination of canid material from Kincaid Shelter (41UV2), located in Uvalde County along the Sabinal River at the southern edge of the Edwards Plateau, demonstrated the presence of a minimum of 4 dogs. Two are from the mixed deposits of looters' back dirt; 1, from the Late Prehistoric Unit 6 deposits; and 1, from the Late Archaic/Late Prehistoric transition at the Unit 5/6 contact (Collins 1990). All 4 are edentulous mandibles broken vertically across the horizontal ramus. Two (1424, 3a) have been burned, and all 4 have cut marks either in the ascending ramus area or ventral horizontal ramus. These cut marks are attributed to butchering techniques in which the mandibular muscles are severed at the attachment with the ramus, and the skin is removed along the jaw prior to fracture for tongue and marrow extraction. Two specimens are fractured between the P4 and M1; 1 between the P3 and P4; and 1 between the P2 and P3. In each case, the marrow cavity was exposed for subsequent marrow extraction.

The Kincaid canids have been identified as *C. familiaris* on the basis of coronoid morphology, ventral horizontal ramus curvature and tooth size/spacing based on alveolar metrics. All 4 mandibles fall within the size range of the more complete Winterbauer dog sample and are also comparable to the Bering specimens. Unlike the other Texas dogs considered in this report, the Kincaid specimens were butchered and presumably consumed.

Dog burials are not common in the major prehistoric mortuary sites on the Gulf Coastal Plain (Hall 1981; Taylor and Highley n.d.). One dog burial was identified at Ernest Witte in the transitional Archaic/

Table 6. *Measurements of Domestic Dog Mandibular Dentitions from Select Sites in Texas*

Site	*M2 Length*	*M2 Width*	*M1 Length*	*M1 Width*	*P4 Length*	*P4 Width*	*P3 Length*	*P3 Width*	*P2 Length*	*P2 Width*	*Canine Length*	*I3 Length*	*I3 Width*
41KR241	7.3ᵃ	6.0	18.1	17.4				9.6	5.0			4.0	3.7
41WD6	8.1	6.0	18.9	8.0	11.2	5.6	10.2	5.0			8.0		
	7.8	6.6	18.3	7.9	9.4	5.3	8.4	4.7					
	8.0	6.6	18.4	8.0	10.4	5.5	9.2	4.4	7.9	4.0	7.7		
	8.0	6.1	19.1	8.4							7.8		
	7.0	6.5	18.8	8.0									
			17.8	7.2									
	7.3	6.2	18.8	7.7	10.2	5.2	8.9	4.3	7.3	3.9			
	8.1	6.3	17.8	6.9									
	8.5	6.9	18.8	8.0	8.9	5.3							
			18.0	7.7									
			17.9	7.4									
				7.0									
41KF7	7.1	6.0	18.2	7.1	9.4	5.0	8.3	4.0	7.1	3.8	7.6		
41UV2			22.5	9.7	12.5	7.0		5.5	9.1	4.6	11.0		
			23.0	7.2									
			18.5	7.0									

ᵃMeasurements are in millimeters.

Late Prehistoric levels (ca. A.D. 550) (Hall 1981:73). The articulated dog was placed in a pit dug for the occasion. The animal was not associated with a human burial. Habitational debris including hearths indicate the site served as a camp as well as a mortuary site.

A dog was also found at the Loevi-Fox site (41WM230) in central Texas (Prewitt 1974). Here, dog remains were recovered from midden debris that postdated the use of this site as a burial ground. The dog material from these sites is consistent with that from a relatively small dog, probably averaging about 14 kilograms, with a head and jaw about the size of a present-day cocker spaniel. Such animals are comparable to the small Indian dog or Pueblo dog as described by Colton (1970:153–159) in the American Southwest. The mummified (desiccated) remains of a small, longhaired black-and-white dog were recovered from a cave in Arizona, illustrating the appearance of some of the small dogs (Colton 1970). The Bering Sinkhole data place this small dog in the central Texas region as early as the Clear Fork Phase (5000–4000 B.P.) of the Archaic period.

Summary of Mammalian Fauna

The excavation of 18 cubic meters of deposits, ranging from 7600 B.P. to the present, from Bering Sinkhole produced mammalian remains of 26 taxa, in addition to humans. Taken as a whole, the faunal assemblage is not significantly different from that found in the central Edwards Plateau region today.

A potentially significant observation is the presence of *Sylvilagus audubonii* in the late Unit III and Unit II deposits (5100–3100 B.P.) dated to the Middle Archaic cultural period during which sinkhole use heightened and again in post-1,000-year-old Unit I deposits after the sinkhole was abandoned. The appearance, disappearance, and then reappearance of *S. audubonii* may be tied to an eastward expansion-retraction-expansion cycle of the *S. audubonii* range identified in the lower Pecos region between 5,000 and 3,000 years ago (Hulbert 1984:204). The expansion is attributed to a period of more xeric conditions on the western Edwards Plateau.

Gophers found on the plateau also contribute to an understanding of past environments. None of the 3 pocket gophers is mapped in the area of Bering Sinkhole today (Davis 1978), although the recovery of their remains in the region indicates favorable habitats were locally available in the not-too-distant past. Recent land use practices that lead to the denudation and erosion of the landscape are probably responsible for their withdrawal from the area.

The recent occurrence of the armadillo follows previously documented patterns as does the post-1000 B.P. presence of *Microtus* sp. The distribution of *Microtus* across the Edwards Plateau since the early Holocene indicates members of this taxon left the central Texas area or were reduced to areas of refuge in the canyon systems by mid-Holocene times (Toomey 1990). The appearance of *Microtus* sp. in the Bering Sinkhole deposits after 1000 B.P. is probably the result of the expansion during periods of ameliorating climatic conditions of the species held in refugium.

Artifacts made of bone, shell, and antler identify a cultural aspect of the sinkhole faunal assemblage. In addition, the recovery of a single mandible and claw of a black bear suggests a human agent was involved.

The recovery of domesticated dogs raised the significant question of whether dogs were intentionally interred in the sinkhole or were victims of a death trap. The data were inconclusive for this problem. The sinkhole deposits also place the small dog in the central Texas region by the Clear Fork Phase (5000–4000 B.P.).

Molluscan Analysis

A sample of snails was obtained from the fine-screen matrix from each of twelve positions in the stratified sequence of the Bering Sinkhole deposits. Analysis of the snails identified 9 terrestrial and 3 freshwater species (Neck 1991; Table 7).

None of the snails are believed to result from cultural activity but were deposited in the sinkhole through natural agents. At present there is no evidence to suggest how the 3 freshwater snail species entered the sinkhole. The snails could have been carried into the sinkhole by raccoons. Only 2 of the terrestrial snails identified in the sinkhole deposits, *Helicodiscus eigenmanni* and *Glyphyalinia roemeri*, inhabit caves and probably established viable populations within Bering Sinkhole (Neck 1991). The remaining species of terrestrial snails probably washed into the sinkhole from the surrounding hill slopes.

All of the species identified at Bering Sinkhole are found on the Edwards Plateau today. The majority of the terrestrial snails are found in habitats ranging from open woodlands and savannahs to grasslands (Neck 1991). Because of the range of climatic tolerance found for each of these species, these snails are of little use in reconstructing paleoclimate. One species, however, provides limited evidence of changing conditions in the vicinity of the sinkhole. The vertical distribution of *Glyphyalinia umbilicata* in the sinkhole deposits suggests that a xeric period occurred between approximately 4000 B.P. and 2700 B.P., matching the data from the rabbits. This xeric period was sufficient to

Table 7 *Freshwater and Terrestrial Snails from Bering Sinkhole*

	Freshwater Snails			Terrestrial Snails		
Level	Planorbula amigero	Gyraulus parvus	Planorbella tenuis	Oligyra orbiculata	Gastrocopta contracta	Helicoduscus eigenmanni
20						
21				1		13
22				5		5
23				2		13
24				3	6	188
25				1		39
26						
27				.3	1	78
28			1			222
29						
30						
31				1		40
32	1			5		255
33						
34						
35		1	1	1		110
36						
37				3		166
38						
39						
40						
41				1		101

extirpate this more mesic adapted snail from the vicinity of the sinkhole. The recovery of this snail in post-2700 B.P. deposits suggests that wetter conditions returned to this portion of the Edwards Plateau.

Summary of Faunal Analysis

The analysis of mammalian and molluscan fauna from Bering Sinkhole yielded information about the succession of animal communities, changing environmental conditions (primarily related to changes in temperature, moisture, and soil depth), and the identification of species with cultural significance. The Bering Sinkhole faunas are representative of Holocene faunas recovered from numerous localities across the Edwards Plateau (Lundelius 1967; Dalquest, Roth, and Judd 1969; Toomey 1990).

| | | | Rabdotus | | |
Helicoduscus singleyanus	Glyphyalinia roemeri	Glyphyalinia umbilicata	dealbatus ragsdalei	Rabdotus mooreanus	Polygyra texasiana
3		7	1		
4	9	1	1		
11	37	3	5		
113	334	5	8		2
40	33	0	5		1
22	127	0	6		
87	204	19	19		
31	80	2	1		
15	20	1	6		
2	86	5	13	4	
19	104			8	
18	49		2		

The rabbit remains suggest the amount of moisture on the Edwards Plateau changed through time, resulting in a mesic interval separating two drying trends. The molluscan fauna supports this shift and signifies that a peak in the drying trend occurred just prior (ca. 3100 B.P.) to the beginning of more mesic conditions after 3000 B.P.

The gophers indicate that the early Holocene saw the greatest soil depth and was followed by the steady erosion of the soil until it had been stripped to the point that virtually all gophers were removed from the area by 1000 B.P.

The inclusion of domestic dogs in the 4,000-to-2,000-year-old deposits is attributed to cultural agents either directly through the intentional placement of dog burials in the site or as a result of the close association dogs maintained with the human population. In the last case, the dogs inadvertently fell into the hole in much the same manner as the coyotes. Bone and antler artifacts provided the identification of the culturally significant fauna in the region. Items of personal adornment were manufactured from the bones of rabbit, turkey, badger, and turtle. Elements of the bear possibly served in a ritual manner as did many of the deer antlers.

7. Artifact Description and Analysis

Bering Sinkhole yielded a wide array of burial goods and incidental inclusions. These materials have been classed according to the artifact types identified at other sites in the region and are presented below according to the material of manufacture.

Lithic Artifacts

The inventory of lithic artifacts lists 88 pieces of chert debitage, 10 dart points, 1 thick biface, 1 thin biface, 1 thin biface fragment, 4 unifaces, 1 unidirectional core, 1 multidirectional core, 1 tested chert cobble, 1 hammerstone/abrader, and a cache of 14 early-stage bifaces and 1 drill/perforator. All measurements are provided in Table 8.

Debitage

Debitage, the refuse from stone tool manufacture, can be divided into reduction categories based on flake morphology and the amount of cortex on the dorsal surface. The Bering debitage sample was sorted using a basic six-part division: primary flakes, secondary flakes, tertiary flakes, pressure flakes, chips, and burned shatter. Flakes are identified by the presence of a striking platform and bulb of percussion. Primary flakes are defined by the presence of cortex on 100 percent of the dorsal surface and on the striking platform. Secondary flakes contain cortex on the dorsal surface or striking platform but do not fit the definition of a primary flake. Secondary flakes, then, have less than 100 percent cortex on the dorsal surface and platform but are not devoid of cortex. Tertiary flakes are defined by the total lack of cortex on both the dorsal flake surface and striking platform. Pressure flakes are small tertiary flakes that have a very thin and narrow platform. These flakes were removed by the application of pressure using a sharp implement to finish shaping the tool. The chip category

Table 8. *Measurements of Lithic Artifacts from Bering Sinkhole*

Artifact Type	Level	Length (cm)	Width (cm)	Thickness (cm)	Figure
Projectile points:					
Frio	0	5.2	4.1	0.1	6a
Burned	24	3.5	2.1	0.8	
Bulverde	27	5.4	3.2	0.6	6b
Travis	28	6.6	1.9	0.7	6c
	31	9.4	2.2	0.8	6d
	31	7.1	1.9	0.7	6e
	31	10.3	2.5	0.8	6f
Uvalde	32	5.9	2.7	0.6	6g
Martindale	39	6.0	3.5	0.6	6h
	36	4.9	3.0	0.7	6i
Bifaces:					
Thin	40	9.2	4.6	1.1	
	26	5.2	3.6	0.6	
Cache:					
Drill	25	9.3	4.2	0.7	7m
Biface 1	25	12.9	6.8	0.9	7a
2	25	14.1	6.0	1.0	7b
3	25	13.3	7.1	1.0	7c
4	25	10.4	6.1	1.1	7d
5	25	13.5	7.0	1.1	7e
6	25	11.3	5.9	1.0	7f
7	25	11.8	7.3	1.0	7g
8	25	12.5	7.2	1.0	7h
9	25	12.3	6.8	0.9	7i
10	25	10.5	5.1	0.9	7j
11	25	10.7	5.6	1.0	7k
12	25	9.1	6.5	1.1	7l
13	25	11.0	6.6	1.2	7n
14	25	13.0	6.7	1.0	7o
Thick unifaces:	29	10.5	6.2	2.0	8c
	38	5.1	6.8	1.7	8a
	36	9.1	5.3	1.5	8b
	34	6.1	4.5	0.5	
	31	3.2	1.7	0.6	
Hammerstone	21	5.2	3.3	2.9	8d
Unidirectional core	26	8.6	6.6	5.2	8e
Multidirectional core	31	8.0	7.0	5.2	
Tested cobble	0	8.2	7.7	3.9	

consists of the medial and distal fragments of flakes and those without a striking platform and bulb of percussion. Burned shatter includes various-sized fragments of chert that have been burned, either intentionally or accidentally.

No primary flakes were recovered from Bering Sinkhole. The debitage consisted of 17 secondary flakes, 26 tertiary flakes, 4 pressure flakes, 20 chips, and 21 pieces of burned shatter. All debitage specimens are of a translucent brown chert with a white chalky cortex where present. The raw material is locally available on the eroded limestone surfaces in the uplands north and east of the sinkhole. Attributes of the striking platform include single- and multiple-faceted platforms on both secondary and tertiary flakes. The small sample size precludes identifying the reduction technology(s) used to produce this debitage.

Dart Points

Frio Dart Point: n = 1.   During the course of the hand excavation, the crew occasionally surveyed the dirt piles left by the track hoe excavation. Eroding from one of the piles purported to be one of the last brought from the hole, was a Frio dart point (Figure 6a). This specimen was missing only the distal tip. The freshness of the fracture suggests that the tip broke during track hoe digging.

This projectile point has straight lateral body edges; deep, upward-trending side notches; and symmetrically placed basal notch. The body is lenticular in cross section. Wide, irregularly placed flake scars on the body are characteristic of tertiary thinning flakes probably removed by soft hammer percussion. The absence of regular-placed pressure flaking suggests that this specimen was not finished at the time of its entry into the sinkhole. The overall shape and notching of this projectile point are characteristic of the Frio dart point style (Turner and Hester 1985:100), a temporal marker aligned with the Uvalde Phase in central Texas by Prewitt (1981).

Burned Dart Point: n = 1.   One badly burned dart point fragment was removed from one of the isolated pockets of charcoal and burned human bone, interpreted as a cremation in Unit I level 24. Burning of the artifact is indicated by the circular fracture patterns on both surfaces of the specimen and the "pot-lid" scars on the surfaces and edges. Beginning at the widest part (midpoint) of the specimen, the distal lateral edges converge gently to what probably was a point. Proximally of the widest portion, the lateral edges constrict abruptly, then parallel one another to what possibly was a straight end or base.

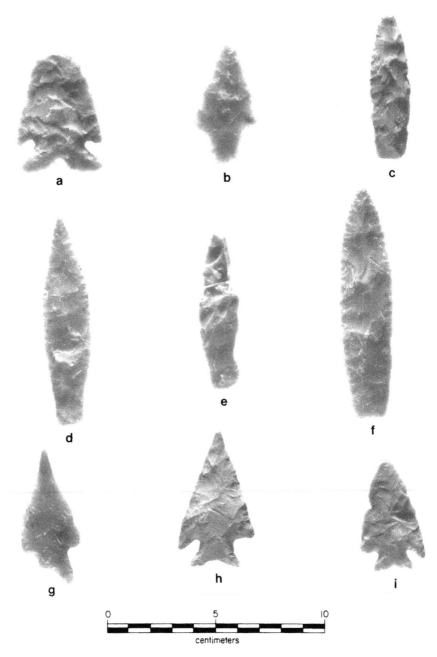

Figure 6. Projectile points recovered from Bering Sinkhole: a, Frio;
b, Bulverde; c–f, lanceolate or Travis; g, Uvalde; h–i, Martindale.

The proximal end is plano-convex in cross section, while the distal end is lenticular to biconvex. The intense fire fracturing precludes its assignment to a specific type of projectile point. Similarly, the color of the chert has been obscured by burning.

Bulverde Dart Point: n = 1.   This well-made artifact has straight blade edges and a lenticular cross section (Figure 6b). The shoulders are asymmetrical: one slants while the other has a short barb. Stem edges contract slightly to a straight, thinned base. The chisellike shape and wedge-shaped longitudinal cross section of the base place this projectile point in the Bulverde type (Turner and Hester 1985:73); however, the contracting stem is atypical. The technological attributes align this specimen with the Bulverde rather than the contracting stem Langtry type. This specimen is made of translucent "rootbeer brown" chert common in the Kerr County area.

Lanceolate Dart Point: n = 4.   Four dart points lacking distinct shoulders were recovered. Two of the points have been reworked; the third and fourth are in pristine form. All four were found in close association with dense accumulations of bone in the Unit II deposits.

One is a roughly fashioned lanceolate projectile point (Figure 6c). The edges of the distal end are worked toward the opposite surface as those of the proximal end—possibly indicating that the blade has been reworked. The base is straight and steeply beveled. This specimen is made of tan chert.

The second specimen has a long, slender body with convex edges and very pointed distal tip (Figure 6d). The edges are slightly serrate, the result of spaced pressure flaking. Shoulders are slight and consist simply of the constriction of the body to the width of the stem. The stem edges and base are straight. The base, although bifacially shaped, is steeply beveled to one surface. This specimen is made of translucent brown chert.

The third is a fragmented projectile point (Figure 6e). The basal portion is lenticular in cross section. The lateral edges are slightly recurved, indicating a slight constriction in the hafting element. The distal portion also is lenticular in cross section. It was removed from the basal portion by a deeply penetrating burinlike fracture originating at the tip. This fracture removed a slender lateral edge, the tip, and penetrated into the basal portion only after initiating a transverse fracture that separated the distal from the proximal end. The base has also been removed by a burinlike fracture, this time initiated along the lateral edge. These breakage patterns are typical of an impact blow, and marks on associated bone indicate that this specimen was embedded in one of the individuals, probably causing death. This specimen is made of opaque brown chert.

The fourth lanceolate point (Figure 6f) is a finely crafted specimen with lenticular cross section, slightly convex lateral edges, straightening in proximity to the haft element, and a straight base. Like the other lanceolate specimens, flaking is perpendicular to the edge, and basal thinning was accomplished by the unifacial beveling of the base preceded by lateral thinning flakes. This specimen is complete. It is made of translucent brown chert.

Shoulderless dart points such as these have been included in the Travis dart point type throughout central Texas (Suhm, Krieger, and Jelks 1954). Similar specimens are illustrated at Stillhouse Hollow (Sorrow, Shafer, and Ross 1967); the Shep site (41KR109) (Luke 1980); and at Canyon Reservoir (Johnson, Suhm, and Tunnell 1962). Other specimens probably belonging to this group have been classified as Angostura points due to their often recurved edges and long, slender lanceolate form. The lack of dulling and grinding of the lateral edges in the area of the haft element, however, suggests these are not Angostura points. Other slender lanceolate bifaces have been classified as "knives" (Sorrow, Shafer, and Ross 1967:25).

Martindale Dart Points: n = 2.   Two projectile points fitting the morphological description of Martindale points (Turner and Hester 1985: 120) have been recovered. These two projectile points have broad bodies with slightly convex edges and lenticular cross sections (Figure 6h, 6i). Shoulders are barbed—the result of corner notching—and each specimen is missing one barb. The stem expands to a concave, fishtail-shaped base. Workmanship on both specimens is excellent. One is made of tan and cream chert, and the second, of cream chert.

Uvalde Dart Point: n = 1.   This specimen (Figure 6g) has a broad body with recurved edges that form a slender point, the result of repeated resharpening. Shoulders are square, although snap fractures on both shoulders may have removed short barbs. The stem, formed by deep corner notches, expands to a bifurcated base. One ear of the deeply notched base is missing; the other is rounded. Morphologically, this specimen fits the Uvalde-type description (Turner and Hester 1985:155). It is made of translucent brown chert.

Bifaces

Thin Biface: n = 1.   This artifact is bifacially fashioned and is subtriangular in outline. The lateral edges are slightly convex, and the base is rounded. A portion of the ventral surface of the large flake on which this artifact was fashioned remains unaltered on one surface. This specimen is made of translucent "rootbeer" brown chert with white inclusions.

Thin Biface Fragments: n = 2.   Two fragments of a single thin biface have been recovered. The partially reconstructed biface consists of a broad, thin triangular blade with slightly convex edges. This portion is plano-convex in cross section and has been fashioned only by the removal of broad percussion flakes. No pressure flaking is evident. One fragment is the distal tip, and the other is the joining midsection to the other fragment. No shoulders are indicated to suggest these fragments are from a projectile point; however, this remains problematical. The breaks resulted in snap fractures, which suggests that they occurred subsequent to the introduction of the artifact into the sinkhole. This means the remaining portions are probably still buried if the artifact was complete upon entry. These fragments are made of orange-red opaque chert.

Cache of Bifaces and Drill/Perforator

DRILL/PERFORATOR: *n* = 1.   The morphology of this specimen suggests that it is a drill/perforator (Figure 7m). The drill bit is 4.50 centimeters long and has a diamond-shaped cross section. The proximal portion is trapezoidal in outline and lenticular in cross section. The drill was fashioned from a triangular preform that had been shaped by pressure flaking. The serrate edge at the junction of the bit and the proximal end suggests that bit fashioning had not been completed. Microscopic examination of the bit did not reveal any usewear on this specimen. This specimen is made of translucent brown chert with tan mottles.

THE BIFACES: *n* = 14.   Biface 1 is subtriangular in outline with rounded basal corners, slightly concave base, and convex lateral edges (Figure 7a). Wide flake scars extend beyond the midline, nearly to the opposite edge. Remnants of platform preparation by perpendicular grinding of the edge are located on narrow protrusions between flake scars. This specimen is made of brown chert with tan mottles.

Biface 2 is triangular in outline with a straight base and slightly convex lateral edges (Figure 7b). Lateral edge flake scars extend across the midline. All edges, including the base, have been ground using both parallel and perpendicular strokes in preparation for additional flake removals. Two flake scars truncate the grinding along one lateral

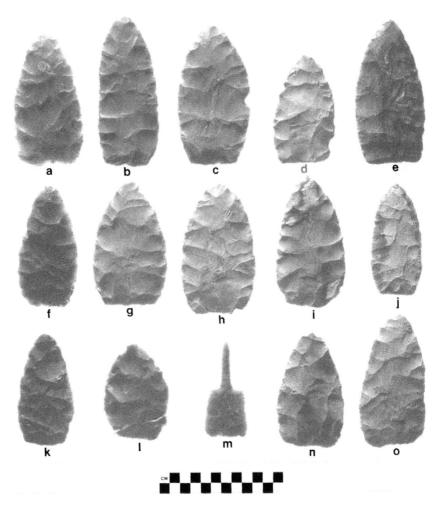

Figure 7. Cache of 14 bifaces (a–l, n–o) and drill/perforator (m) from Bering Sinkhole.

edge. This specimen is made of a banded honey-brown and purple chert with a waxy luster, suggesting possible heat treatment.

Biface 3 is triangular in outline with a straight base and convex lateral edges (Figure 7c). Broad flake scars terminate at midline. Parallel grinding of the edge for platform preparation is disrupted by flake removal, leaving only small protrusions on either side of platform scars. This specimen is made of light brown chert with yellow inclusions.

Biface 4 is triangular in outline with a straight base and convex edges (Figure 7d). Flake scars extend beyond the midline. Perpendicular grinding of the bifacial edge is indicated on the protrusions between flake scars. This specimen is made of tan chert with gray and translucent honey-brown patches along one edge.

Biface 5 is triangular in outline with a slightly concave base and convex lateral edges (Figure 7e). The majority of flake scars terminate at midline, although a few extend beyond. The entire periphery has been ground using both perpendicular and parallel strokes. The grinding is continuous—not truncated by postgrinding flake removal. This specimen is made of grayish brown chert with tan, cream, and black mottles.

Biface 6 is subtriangular in outline with a straight base, rounded corners, and convex lateral edges (Figure 7f). A patch of white chalky cortex remains on one basal corner. Numerous flake scars extend across the midline. Flake scars truncate the perpendicular ground edges. This specimen is made of translucent brown chert with cream-colored mottles.

Biface 7 is triangular in outline with a straight base and convex lateral edges (Figure 7g). Numerous flake scars extend beyond the midline. Light perpendicular grinding of the biface edge has been disrupted by the removal of flakes. This specimen is made of translucent light brown chert with a slight waxy luster suggestive of heat treatment.

Biface 8 is triangular in outline with a concave base and convex edges (Figure 7h). Wide flake scars terminate beyond the midline. Grinding of the edges by parallel and perpendicular motion has been truncated by the subsequent removal of flakes. This specimen is made of tan chert with translucent inclusions.

Biface 9 is triangular in outline with a straight base and convex lateral edges (Figure 7i). Numerous flake scars extend beyond the midline. The removal of flakes truncated edge grinding oriented parallel with the edge. This specimen is made of tan chert with coarse-textured cream-colored veins.

Biface 10 is triangular in outline with a straight base and convex lateral edges (Figure 7j). Flake scars terminate at the midline and truncate edge preparation of perpendicular and parallel grinding. This specimen is made of banded yellow and brown chert with a cream-colored cortexlike seam down the midline.

Biface 11 is subtriangular in outline with a slightly convex base and convex lateral edges (Figure 7k). Numerous scars terminate beyond the midline. Parallel grinding of the bifacial edge extends around the entire periphery of the biface. This specimen is made of a mottled brown and dark brown chert.

Biface 12 is triangular in outline with convex lateral edges and a straight base beveled toward one surface (Figure 7l). Flake scars terminate at the midline. Edge preparation is indicated by the remnants of perpendicularly ground edges on either side of flake scars. Biface 12 was trapped on an undulating limestone block surface directly beneath the proximal end. Pressure from overburden caused the specimen to snap in a transverse fracture. The fracture occurred one-quarter the length from the proximal end. This specimen is made of dark brown chert with a small patch of white chalky cortex along an edge near the distal tip and opposite basal corner.

Biface 13 is triangular in outline with a concave base and convex lateral edges (Figure 7n). Flake scars terminate at midline, and a long, broad basal thinning scar traverses two-thirds the length of the biface. Remnants of platform preparation by perpendicular and parallel grinding of the edge are identifiable on narrow protrusions between the flake scars. This specimen is made of light brown chert with cream and light brown mottles.

Biface 14 is subtriangular in outline with a slightly concave base, rounded corners, and convex edges (Figure 7o). Some flake scars extend beyond the midline. Both parallel and perpendicular grinding of the biface edge is indicated by remnants between flake scars. This specimen is made of tan chert with brown patches. A patch of cortex is retained on one basal corner.

Thick Biface: n = 1. This artifact is pointed at both ends and has convex lateral edges (Figure 8c). It is a large secondary flake that has been bifacially reduced, although cortex still covers approximately one-fourth of the dorsal surface, and the bulb of percussion is visible on one end. This specimen is at an early stage in the reduction sequence. It is made of tan chert.

Uniface: n = 4. The first, a utilized flake, is made on a corticate secondary flake (Figure 8a). The specimen is subtriangular in outline; the striking platform is located at the apex; and the working edge is at the base. The thickest portion of the tool is along the working face. No formal edge preparation is present, although step fractures along the edge indicate this flake was used as a scraper. This specimen is made of translucent brown and tan chert.

The second artifact is a large, cortex platform secondary flake that has had the distal end shaped into a point by unifacial pressure flaking of the dorsal surface (Figure 8b). The distal one-half of one edge is straight as well as the distal one-quarter of the intersecting lateral edge. This specimen is made of gray chert.

Figure 8. Additional lithic artifacts from Bering Sinkhole: a–b, unifaces; c, thick biface; d, hammerstone/abrader; e, unidirectional core.

The third uniface is a thin, single-faceted platform secondary flake that has been fashioned into a side scraper. This artifact is made of brown chert.

A fourth specimen is a small segment of a unifacially flaked edge of a much larger artifact. The fragment is biplane in cross section. This fragment is made of translucent brown chert.

Hammerstone/Abrader: n = 1.   This artifact is a small chertlike nodule with thick limestone cortex (Figure 8d). Three facets with longitudinal striations have been worn into the cortex. The striations are probably the result of platform grinding of biface edges during platform preparation in anticipation of further reduction. Three additional facets have been worn by battering attributable to the reduction process, a result of percussion flaking employed during platform preparation.

Unidirectional Core: n = 1.   This specimen is a conical unidirectional core fashioned from a tabular cobble (Figure 8e). The removal of a single large primary flake created a single-faceted platform from which numerous flakes and blades have been sequentially struck around one-half the circumference of the core. The core is made on cream and brown mottled chert.

Multidirectional Core: n = 1.   This specimen is a chert cobble that has been reduced by the removal of numerous flakes from various striking platforms. Cleavage planes in the cobble, however, caused the core to fracture in an angular and unpredictable manner. The core is made of translucent brown and tan chert.

Tested Chert Cobble: n = 1.   This specimen is a rectangular tabular chert cobble with cortex on both surfaces and along two edges. The remaining two sides are fractured, exposing fine-grained tan chert. The scars on the exposed chert are covered with a mottled white patina.

Bone, Antler, Shell, and Turtle Carapace Artifacts

Bone Awl: n = 2.   The first awl is fashioned from the right proximal ulna of a small deer, probably white-tailed (Figure 9a). The olecranon is fractured but appears to have remained unaltered and served as a handle. The shaft has been tapered to a point, although the sharpened end is broken.

The second specimen is fashioned from a split metapodial of a deer-sized animal (Figure 9b). The epiphyseal end is missing or was removed. The medullar cavity is stripped of all cancellous material and the entire artifact is smoothed and polished. Six paired thin lines on the dorsal surface run parallel to the long axis of the artifact. The distal end tapers dramatically to a long slender tip with a circular cross section. Low-power microscopy failed to identify patterned wear that would suggest the function of the implement.

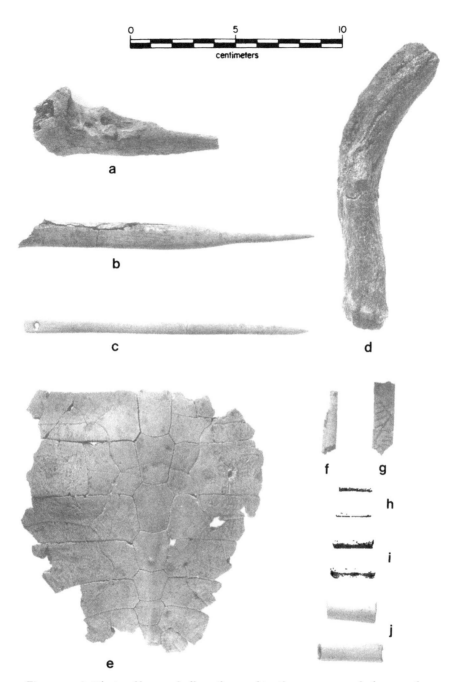

Figure 9. Artifacts of bone, shell, antler, and turtle carapace: a–b, bone awls; c, bone pin; d, antler billet; e, turtle carapace bowl or hair ornament; f, incised bone pin fragment; g, incised bone implement; h–j, rabbit and turkey bone beads.

Bone Pin: n = 1.   This implement is made entirely of cortical bone reduced by longitudinal abrasion (Figure 9c). The length and thickness of the implement suggest that a deer metapodial was the source of the bone, although antelope or larger animals could also have supplied the blank. The tip is lenticular in cross section, and microscopic examination showed no transverse markings to suggest the tool was used in a twisting motion. The longitudinal striae are more indicative of a batonlike weaving use. The proximal end is perforated using a back-and-forth twisting action from both surfaces, rendering an elliptical hole 1.8 millimeters long by 2.5 millimeters wide. The entire artifact has an approximate one-sixteenth counterclockwise torque.

Incised Bone Pin Fragment: n = 1.   This specimen is a segment of a tapering bone implement with an oval cross section (Figure 9f). The surface treatment, including longitudinally oriented smoothing striations, suggests it is a segment of a bone pin. In addition, numerous evenly spaced parallel oblique-incised hatches cover half the circumference, and the remaining area is covered by chevronlike incisions.

Incised Bone Implements: n = 4.   Four segments of thin, narrow batonlike bone implements the size and configuration of popsicle sticks have been recovered (Figure 9g). The four are made from thick cortical bone of undetermined source, although deer-sized long bones could have been used. Each fragment is decorated by an incised zigzag line. The resulting spaces bordered by the line are further incised with three to five short bars oriented perpendicular to the bone edge. In addition, one fragment has an incised line on the opposite face, but the specimen is too small to suggest a design. The variation in execution of design, variance in the width and thickness, and their stratigraphic positioning suggest that four different batons are represented. Three are from Unit II level 27, and the fourth is from Unit II level 25.

Bone implements with incised decorations have been found across the state of Texas, and many have been recovered from burial contexts on the Gulf Coastal Plain (Hall 1981, 1988; Taylor and Highley n.d.). These implements are assigned such functions as hair pins, piercing awls, weaving awls, sweat scrapers, and louse crushers, based on ethnographic and morphologic determinations. The design elements may have functioned as group identifiers (Hall 1988) or as marks to be interpreted during games or divinations (Dewez 1974).

Although the majority of the reported bone pins have been found in caches or stacks lying beside a burial, three such implements from the Ernest Witte site were recovered under the skulls of people, suggesting that these served as hair pins (Hall 1981). Other sites where the implements have been found in association with skulls include Olmos Dam (Lukowski 1988), Green Lake (Wingate and Hester 1972), and Brandes (Highley et al. 1988).

The Bering specimens are too incomplete to accurately project their size and shape. However, their dimensions indicate they are on the small end of the range of the implements discussed by Hall (1988).

Bone Beads: n = 294. A total of 294 bone beads and 1 bone bangle have been recovered from the excavations to date. The beads are tubular segments of rabbit and turkey long bones or the shafts of mammal metatarsals (Figure 9h, 9i, and 9j).

BEAD MANUFACTURE. All beads were made using the groove and snap technique. In this technique, a long bone is prepared by first removing the articular ends by incising or sawing grooves around the circumference of the shaft. Two or three grooves, barely penetrating the medullar cavity, are cut. The ends are snapped off by grasping the bone on both sides of the groove and prying or bending with a sudden exertion of force.

Once the ends are removed, the shaft is abraded to a smooth, polished luster. Abrasion grooves, extending onto the incisions at the distal and proximal shaft ends, indicate that epiphyseal removal preceded polishing. However, midshaft grooves truncate abrasion marks, thus polishing took place prior to the segmentation of the shaft into bead segments. The majority of the beads were not further altered once the shaft had been segmented. However, the ends of several beads were smoothed to the extent that grooves are obliterated.

The majority of the beads are made from the femur or tibia of cottontail rabbits (*Sylvilagus* sp.); 39 beads are made of turkey ulna bones; and the remainder are rabbit metatarsals.

A single rabbit femur or tibia could produce 3 beads averaging 18.9 millimeters in length. Thus, each rabbit could supply 12 beads. Using a minimum number of 18 rabbits (calculated by the number of tibia midsections), a total of 216 beads could have been made. Each rabbit could also contribute 8 metatarsals of sufficient size for beads, thus adding another potential 144 beads. Of the 294 beads from the sinkhole, 253 are from rabbits. This total is well below the 360 beads possible from the 18 rabbits. Of course, probably not all possible beads were made, nor is it likely that only 18 rabbits were used in making the beads in the sinkhole, nor is it likely that all beads in the sinkhole have been recovered. These calculations are presented simply to provide a basis for the bead technology represented at the sinkhole.

A more striking statistic is that the 294 beads, placed end to end, would create a single strand 6 meters (19.7 feet) long. The concentrations of beads in level 22 of excavation units m and k would create an estimated strand 1.5 and 1.1 meters long, respectively.

The bone bangle is fashioned on the proximal half of the left radius of a badger (*Taxidea taxus*). The epiphyseal end was not removed, and the radius was truncated by the groove and snap technique. Polish and shallow abrasions in the natural fossa between the epiphysis and radial tuberosity indicate the bone was attached to a necklace or bracelet by a narrow thong or string.

DISTRIBUTION OF BEADS.   Bone beads were found in levels 22 through 29, most occurring in levels 23, 24, 25, and 27. These levels are on either side of the depositional break between the black clay of Unit I and the brown clay of Unit II.

Although it is recognized that the small size of the beads ($x = 18.9$ millimeters) makes them prime candidates for vertical movement, their presence on both sides of a distinct depositional boundary suggests that identical technology and use were components of a cultural tradition that utilized the sinkhole before, during, and after the climatic shift indicated by the depositional changes—a span of nearly 1,000 years.

Deer Antler Billet: n = 1.   A fragment of deer antler was recovered in association with the human skeletal remains. The antler fragment is composed of the beam of the antler from its base to 5 centimeters beyond the eye tine (Figure 9d). The tine had been removed flush with the beam, and the crenellations at the base of the antler beam have been removed for the majority of the circumference. The distal end of the antler fragment is rounded, removing any sign of the means of cutting or breakage. A facet tangential to the truncation on the inside curve of the beam is similar to the striking facet identified on billet punches and hammers (Michaels 1987:115). This facet forms as a result of percussion with stone material, suggesting this antler fragment was intentionally fashioned and used as a soft hammer or billet probably in the production (reduction) of flaked stone tools. The small size of this tool, 12.9 centimeters long, 3.0 centimeters wide, 1.9 centimeters thick, and 45.2 grams weight perhaps indicates that this billet was used in the final shaping or reduction of thin lithic tools (e.g., projectile points).

Deer Antler Segments: n = 39.   A total of 39 deer antler fragments have been recovered from the sinkhole deposits. They consist of portions of the beams, tips, and bases of shed antlers and range in length from 3 centimeters to 28 centimeters. The actual size and number of antlers represented by these fragments is unknown. Even the large beam fragments (up to 4 centimeters in diameter) are in a poor state of preservation. However, it is assumed that at least some of these fragments entered the sinkhole as complete antler halves. In one instance, basal portions of both antlers are still attached to a segment of the skull. Thirteen of the antler fragments have been burned. Although these are tentatively identified as white-tailed deer antlers, none of the fragments retained diagnostic elements to rule out mule deer.

With the exception of two small fragments from Unit III levels 38 and 36, antler was restricted to Unit II levels 29 through 25 and Unit I level 24. Within this distribution, burned antler was found mixed with nonburned fragments in levels 27 through 25, but composed the entire sample from level 24.

Modified Turtle Carapace: n = 1.   The carapace of a Texas slider (*Pseudemys concina texana* or *Chrysemys concina texana*) has been altered to form a bowl, scoop, or hair ornament. This specimen consists of the neural, nuchal, suprapygal, and several peripheral bone plates (Figure 9e). The dorsal vertebrae, fused to the neural plates in adults, have been removed along with the ribs that attached to the costal plates. All fused contact points of the ribs and dorsal vertebrae have been abraded flush with the visceral surfaces of the neural and costal plates. Striae from the grinding and smoothing indicate that an alternating anterior/posterior motion was employed.

In addition, the edges of many of the peripheral plates have been abraded either through use or shaping the artifact. Likewise, the apex of the outer (dorsal) surface of the carapace is highly polished along the second through fifth neurals and adjacent portions of the costal plates. This polish consists of randomly oriented abrasions and apparently is the result of resting the artifact on the ground like a bowl. The presence of polish on the bony plates indicates the thin shields that cover the outer shell were removed or had fallen off during the use-life of the artifact. The association of this artifact with the long, slender bone pin suggests the possibility that the two items functioned together as a hair ornament, the bone being inserted through the gaps between the costal and peripheral plates, holding the hair in place.

No mastic residues were found to suggest that a sealant had been applied to waterproof the sutures between the plates, although none is needed on an adult shell unless a crack or hole develops.

This specimen was approximately 20 centimeters long, 16 centime-

Table 9 *Identification and Distribution of Freshwater Mussel Species from Bering Sinkhole*

Taxon	Unit/Level
Quincuncina mitchelli (2 halves)	II/31, III/37
Megalonaias nervosa	III/37
Lampsilis teres (3 halves)	III/37, 38, 39
Amblema plicata	III/37
Uniomerus declivus	III/40

ters wide, and could hold up to 400 milliliters of a liquid or twice that of a dry substance that would not fall through the gaps between the costal and peripheral plates.

Freshwater Mussel Shell: n = 8. Eight halves of freshwater mussel shells were contained in the burial lenses. These have been identified as belonging to various taxa, all of which can be found in the Guadalupe or Llano river systems today (Table 9; Neck 1991).

The mussel shells have a very limited distribution in the sinkhole, only one specimen being from above the Unit III deposits. Although available in the nearby river systems today, there is no source in the valley margin setting of the sinkhole.

Marine Shell Pendants: n = 2. Two marine shell pendants were recovered along with one thin biface in the lower portion of Unit III. These pendants are made from the whelk (*Busycon* sp.). The first is fashioned from the outer whorl (Figure 10, upper), and the second, from the columella or central pillar of the shell (Figure 10, lower). Both have a single hole drilled through the surfaces. The whorl pendant is subtriangular, the hole drilled at the apex. This specimen is 9.0 centimeters long, 4.7 centimeters wide, and 0.6 centimeter thick. The other pendant was formed on a longitudinally split columella that was subsequently ground into a rectangular tablet. This specimen is 8.4 centimeters long, 2.0 centimeters wide, and 0.7 centimeter thick.

Marine Shell Beads: n = 17. Seventeen beads, 16 made from the small *Olivella dealbata* and 1 from the *Olivella minuta*, were fashioned by the removal of the spire of the shell by abrasion. The *O. dealbata* beads range in size from 5.25 millimeters long and 3.15 millimeters in diameter to 8.5 millimeters long and 3.85 millimeters in diameter. The *O. minuta* is 8.35 millimeters long and 5.80 millimeters in diameter. These mollusks range from North Carolina to Florida along the Atlan-

Figure 10. Front and back views of marine shell pendants from Bering Sinkhole.

tic Ocean and from Florida to Texas in the Gulf of Mexico. Large numbers of shells of these species have been reported along Texas beaches
during the winter, particularly after a storm (Andrews 1981:60).

Cultural Implications of the Bering Sinkhole Artifact Assemblage

The artifacts described above have important implications in reconstructing the use of Bering Sinkhole as a burial locus over time. The
projectile points provide temporal data to supplement and corroborate the dating of the deposits obtained by radiocarbon assay, as well
as providing a means to link the burials with their contemporary societies that are best recognized on the basis of projectile point mor-
phologies. The vertical distribution and association of the various artifacts provide clues to the burial furnishings deemed appropriate by
the different cultures through time and to any implications derived
from the form and number of these inclusions.

Chronological Implications

The projectile points corroborate and extend the chronology of site
use shown by radiocarbon assays. The Martindale, Uvalde, Travis,
Bulverde, and Frio dart points carry chronological implications. Using
Weir's (1976) cultural chronology, these projectile points are diagnostic of the San Geronimo, Clear Fork, Round Rock, and Twin Sisters
phases, respectively. Of course, these are not the only phases represented by burial components in the sinkhole, only those that included
projectile points of defined affiliation. These projectile points substantiate both the dating of the burial lenses by radiocarbon assays of
charcoal from either cremations or associated ritual activity, and the
ages arrived at by accretion rates of the sedimentary units (Table 10).

Assemblage Reconstruction

Since the projectile points are in stratigraphically correct position, the
other artifacts can be placed in a temporal framework. Those artifacts
that are found in close proximity to each other, whether horizontally
or vertically, will be considered components of a burial assemblage.
To this end, the various artifacts were grouped according to the 10-
centimeter-thick analytical levels. Certain anomalies in the natural
accretion of the deposits, such as the inclusion of numerous large
limestone blocks in the Unit III deposits, suggest that certain of the
artifacts recovered in stratigraphically adjacent arbitrary units probably are parts of the same assemblage. Given the limitations imposed

Table 10. *Distribution of Projectile Point Types Recovered from Bering Sinkhole (proposed ages of analysis levels and 14C dates in calendrical years B.P.)*

	Level	Age Range (cal. yrs. B.P.)	Associated C-14 Assays	Dart Points
Unit I	19	790–1175	(Tx-6525, Pitt 0073)	
	20	1175–1560		
	21	1560–1945		
	22	1945–2330	(Tx-6921)	
	23	2330–2715		
	24	2715–3100	(Tx-5877, Tx-6167)	
Unit II	25	3100–3400		
	26	3400–3700	(Tx-6135)	
	27	3700–3980		Bulverde
	28	3980–4260		Travis
	29	4260–4540		
	30	4540–4820		
	31	4820–5100		Travis
Unit III	32	5100–5380		Uvalde
	33	5380–5660		
	34	5660–5940		
	35	5940–6220		
	36	6220–6500		Martindale
	37	6500–6780	(Tx-6282)	
	38	6780–7050		
	39	7050–7320		Martindale
	40	7320–7590	(Tx-6831, Tx-6526)	
	41	7590–7760		
Unit IV	42	Pleistocene?		

by the often variable depositional incongruities, these general components will be discussed according to temporal units defined by Weir (1976). As noted often above, the dispersed condition of the burials precludes the identification and association of the artifacts with any specific burial.

The sinkhole was first used by humans during the San Geronimo Phase (Weir 1976). Deposits that roughly correspond to this period include Unit III levels 32 through 41. A radiocarbon date in level 41 provides a maximum age for the cultural deposits of 7500 B.P. Thus, the sinkhole was used during the latter portion of the San Geronimo Phase, roughly dated between 7500 and 5100 B.P. Artifacts in these levels are 2 marine shell pendants, 1 biface, 7 unaltered mussel shells,

1 deer ulna awl, 2 Martindale dart points, 1 modified turtle carapace, 1 bone needle, 1 thin uniface, 1 pointed uniface, 1 uniface/biface edge, and 1 Uvalde dart point. Of the artifacts, only the Martindale and Uvalde dart points are considered temporal markers.

The Clear Fork Phase is represented by the brown sediments of Unit II levels 28 through 31. Artifacts recovered from these levels are 4 Travis dart points, 1 bone awl, 1 unmodified mussel shell, 1 utilized flake uniface, 1 multidirectional core, 1 incised pin tip, 1 biface, and deer antler. The Travis and Nolan dart points are considered temporal markers for the Clear Fork Phase (Prewitt 1981, 1985).

The sinkhole deposits of the Round Rock Phase are Unit I level 24 and Unit II levels 25, 26, and 27. Contained within these deposits were 1 Bulverde dart point, 2 incised bone batons, 1 thin biface (2 parts), 1 unidirectional core, deer antler, 17 marine olivella shell beads, 14 bifaces (cache), 1 drill (in cache), 1 incised bone baton, numerous bone beads, and 1 burned dart point.

The Bulverde dart point is an accepted temporal marker for this phase and is usually accompanied by Pedernales points (Weir 1976; Prewitt 1981, 1985). The burned dart point is untypable. The varied kinds of artifacts recovered from these deposits are considered more fully in the next section and then again in the final chapter.

Portions of Unit I levels 22 and 23 correspond to the San Marcos Phase. The only artifacts from these two levels are tubular bone beads. In addition, a single radiocarbon date providing an age range between 2303 and 2021 B.P. (Tx-6921) was obtained from charcoal with a cremation.

The final period represented in the sinkhole is the Twin Sisters Phase. Unit I levels 20 and 21 are dated to this period. These levels contained numerous tubular bone beads and 1 hammerstone/abrader. The Frio dart point recovered from the track hoe back dirt pile is probably from these levels.

Artifacts and Mortuary Practices

The items in the sinkhole can be classed as either utilitarian, personal adornment, or ritual items. Items of personal adornment are the marine shell pendants, olivella beads, bone beads, bone bangle, bone pins possibly used for hair pins, and the turtle shell hair ornament. Utilitarian items are the unifaces, bifaces, projectile points, hammerstone/abrader, drill, antler billet, cores, and bone awls.

Problematic items that are not easily classified are the burned and unburned deer antler fragments and the incised bone batons. All of these items may have mundane roles: for instance, the antlers could have been raw material for flakers, and the bone batons could have been hair pins, sweat scrapers, or louse crushers. On the other hand, these items may have had ritualized functions.

Debitage and pieces of burned rock are classified as incidental inclusions and were probably not purposefully introduced into the sinkhole. Debitage, which is lightly scattered on the hill slopes above the sinkhole, probably washed in as did much of the small limestone class of the sediments. Burned rock was probably bundled with cremations. The burned dart point could be considered an incidental inclusion as could the projectile point that was imbedded in an individual.

All items not considered incidental inclusions, whether they are utilitarian or personal adornment, undergo a transference (transformation) from the realm of the mundane into that of the sacred upon entering the sinkhole. Such artifacts are consecrated through ritual. And it is through the patterned inclusion of some of these materials that Bartel's (1982) inverse black box paradox can be avoided.

The cache of large bifaces and drill provided the opportunity to test the proposition that large numbers of artifacts are the product of group contributions and, as such, represent group investment in the burial of the dead (Bement 1991). To determine if more than one flintknapper was responsible for the cache, the 14 bifaces were analyzed according to technological and idiosyncratic attributes. If it could be shown that all the bifaces were at the same technological stage in the reduction process, then any variances in nontechnical attributes could be attributed to the idiosyncrasies of different flintknappers. To this end, the statistical analyses of cluster and discriminant function were applied to a data set of ten technological and six idiosyncratic variables obtained for each biface.

Cluster analysis of idiosyncratic variables produced three groups of bifaces. Discriminant function analysis employing technological variables indicates that all bifaces were at the same stage in the bifacial reduction sequence and that there were no significant technological differences among the three groups. Thus, these analyses support the proposition that the differences among the biface groups are attributable to idiosyncratic behavior. It is concluded that at least three flintknappers were responsible for the manufacture of the bifaces contained in the cache.

Biface blanks such as these have been recovered in burial contexts in sites to the east and south, at distances over 300 kilometers. The recovery of similar biface blanks in mortuary sites on, as well as off, the Edwards Plateau indicates the sanctification of the exchange network and the importance of this network in the social structure at both ends of the exchange. The recovery of marine shell beads in the same level as that containing the biface cache suggests that one end of the exchange network was near the Gulf Coast. The recovery of large bifaces at Loma Sandia, a large mortuary site south of the Edwards Plateau and on the Coastal Plain further strengthens this inference.

8. Bioarchaeology

The remains of an estimated 62 individuals, including at least 6 cremations and 1 bundle burial were recovered from Bering Sinkhole. In addition to providing basic descriptive information (age, sex, stature) about local central Texas Archaic inhabitants, the bioarchaeological analysis presented here concentrates on the identification of stress-related characteristics of the skeletons that may indicate shifts in subsistence, mobility, and technology. Such indicators are hypoplasia rates, caries rates, occlusal wear patterns, and stable isotope configurations. To facilitate the interpretation of the results of these various analyses, the skeletal remains are grouped according to the macro time intervals of Weir's (1976) phase chronology: San Geronimo, Clear Fork, Round Rock, San Marcos, and Twin Sisters. These results are compared to those obtained for other Archaic skeletal series from sites on the Gulf Coastal Plain, the lower Pecos region of Texas, and various sites in North America.

The bioarchaeological analysis is divided into four parts: taphonomy, paleodemography, paleoepidemiology, and paleodiet.

Taphonomy

The human skeletal remains were subjected to many of the same destructive forces as were evidenced in the nonhuman remains described in chapter 6. Three of the most active agents were rodent gnawing, water action, and root etching. Humans are responsible for the placement and perhaps partial burial of human corpses in the sinkhole. Preburial treatment, including the cremation of six and natural defleshing of one, was performed prior to placement of the remains in the sinkhole. The majority, however, are thought to have been fully fleshed and articulated when dropped or lowered onto the debris cone under the opening. The correlation of large limestone blocks and burials suggests that some attempt was made to cover or conceal the corpses. The extent to which tossed rocks impacted the skeletal material is unknown, since the majority of the bones were fractured prior to excavation, and other destructive forces were at work in the sinkhole.

Approximately 20 percent of both human and nonhuman bone from each level bears the characteristic grooves of small rodent gnawing. Prominent ridges and epiphyseal ends were favorite targets for gnawing. No evidence was found to suggest that animals larger than a woodrat were responsible for the destruction. No punctures characteristic of carnivore chewing were found on any of the human or, for that matter, nonhuman remains.

Root etching was rarely observed. The upper cone deposits produced the bulk of root disturbance including roots penetrating long bones.

Water, originating as runoff after rainstorms, affected the skeletal material by the disarticulation and distribution of elements. The recovery of articulated segments, primarily hands and feet, but also including a nearly complete torso, indicates that some corpses were at least partially protected from destructive agents. In similar fashion, the neat stack of long bones interpreted as a bundle burial suggests that a bag or wrapping protected these bones. Burial was accomplished through the apparent practice of throwing limestone blocks into the opening, followed by the natural sedimentation of silts and clays by surface runoff.

The end result of these various processes, then, was the commingling and differential destruction of skeletal elements from multiple interments that, owing to the continuous and fairly rapid rate of sedimentation, are in stratified contexts.

Paleodemography

Paleodemographic data derived here are of three sorts: minimum number of individuals (MNI) contained in the sinkhole deposits, age distribution of the burial populations, and sex distribution.

Determination of MNI

The track hoe pit produced the remains of a MNI of 9 individuals, based on counts of the right distal humeri (McIntosh 1988). Although more than one level of burials is represented, the lack of provenience precluded segregating the sample. The track hoe pit did not penetrate into the Unit II brown deposits, so the sample is from the Unit I, levels 20–23 burials of the Late Archaic (2600–2000 B.P.).

Marks (1991) distinguished a MNI of 37 from units a through j by using the right distal end of the humerus, the petrous, and cremated remains. The Unit k–o sample contained an estimated 13 individuals based on the number of right distal humeri. In addition, the recovery of portions of 1 cremated and 1 noncremated individual from the top of Unit k and a calcified fetus in the nonhuman remains from Unit c increases the total to 16. The total MNI recovered from the site is 62.

Unlike Seminole Sink, where the entire human burial deposits were excavated and the MNI corresponded to the total individuals in the cavern, the Bering Sinkhole MNI represents a sampling of approximately half of the depositional cone directly under the opening and a small fraction of the deposits extending along the long axis of the cavern. Thus, the MNI could represent as much as 50 percent of the sinkhole population or as little as 25 percent. The change through time in debris cone morphology affected the distribution and ultimate burial of skeletal material. As a result, some levels were most productive on the cone surface directly under the opening, while others were most productive along the edges of the debris cone. For example, the Unit III level 38 deposits yielded the remains of 2 individuals from directly under the opening and an additional 3 persons at the edge of the cone to the north, while Unit I level 24 yielded 6 individuals under the opening and only 1 individual to the north. Although not all of the skeletal remains have been removed from the sinkhole, the sample recovered to date is thought to be large enough to provide analysis results representative of each cultural time period. If the MNI represents 50 percent of the sinkhole burial population, then a conservative total of 124 individuals is estimated at this site.

Vertical Distribution of Burials

The distribution of long bones was used to define the burial zones. Smaller elements are more prone to vertical and horizontal movement. Because of the lack of provenience, the 9 individuals recovered by the track hoe (McIntosh 1988) were not included in the distributional analysis. The plot of numbers of individuals by level produces a pattern of episodic use of the sinkhole through time. The most recent use of the sinkhole as a burial locus was in level 20, and the oldest burials are in level 40. Levels containing the most individuals are 24, 31, 32, 35, and 38 with counts of 7, 7, 5, 6, and 5 burials, respectively. No distal humeri were found in levels 21, 27, 30, 33, or

34. Although other skeletal elements were recovered from these levels, bone density was lowest in levels not containing distal humeri.

Age and Sex

The techniques employed to determine the sex of the individuals were the shape of the sciatic notch on pelves, measurements of the distal humerus, circumference of the femur diaphysis, cranial attributes, and mandible robustness (Bass 1987; Brothwell 1981; Steele and Bramblett 1988). Due to the disarticulated condition of the skeletons, it was not possible to determine if various elements in the same analysis level belonged to a single individual or to several individuals. In addition, the sexing methods apply only to adult remains. The resultant sex distribution suggests that, overall, equal numbers of adult males and females were placed in the sinkhole (Table 11).

Age determinations of the sinkhole population were also hampered by the disarticulated and dispersed condition of the skeletons. As with sexing, age determination is best estimated by comparing various cranial and postcranial features. When the various elements could not be attributed to specific individuals, age determinations were less exact. Among the factors considered in the determination of the age of the sinkhole individuals were tooth eruption patterns, cranial suture closure, stage of epiphyseal fusion on postcranial elements, and length of long bones on infants (Steele and Bramblett 1988; Bass 1987; Brothwell 1981; Fazekas and Kosa 1978).

The high attrition rate of the molar occlusal surfaces and further alterations due to using the mouth in the processing of some material (see below) precluded the use of dental wear patterns in the determination of age. Although roughly two-thirds of the individuals from the sinkhole were adults, the subadults displayed more characteristics that could be used in determining the age at death. Again, these attributes were tooth eruption patterns and epiphyseal fusion of postcranial elements.

The burial population for the San Geronimo Phase (Unit III levels 40–32) contained 8 subadults ranging in age from 1 to 9 years old and 15 adults ranging in age from 20 to 50 years old. Age distribution of the Clear Fork Phase (Unit II levels 31–28) population included 4 subadults, including 1 less than 1 year old, 1 between 1 and 2 years old, 1 between 2 and 3 years old, 1 between 12 and 13 years old, and 7 adults ranging in age between 25 and 50 years old. Round Rock Phase (Unit II levels 27–25 and Unit I level 24) age distribution included 4 subadults ranging from fetus to 15 years old and 7 adults ranging from 20 to over 45 years old. During the San Marcos Phase (Unit I

Table 11 *Distribution of Sexed Individuals from Bering Sinkhole*

	Male	Female
Twin Sisters	Unknown	Unknown
San Marcos	2	2
Round Rock	4	4
Clear Fork	3	4
San Geronimo	2	1
Total	11	11

levels 22–23), burials included 3 subadults between the ages of 1 and 7 and 3 adults. The Twin Sisters Phase (Unit I levels 20–21) burials were of 2 adults.

Of the 6 cremations, all were adults and at least 3 were male (Marks 1991). The sex could not be determined on the remaining 4. Similarly, the single bundle burial is that of an adult, but in this case the individual was female based on the biepicondylar width and articular width of the humerus and the circumference of the femur midshaft (Bass 1987:219).

Stature

The estimation of stature of the population was hampered by the fractured condition of the long bones. Only in instances where the long bones were encased in spray foam (Bement 1985a) prior to removal was it possible to estimate the length of the bones for use in determining the stature. Measurements from three adult femurs and 1 adult tibia rendered stature estimates ranging from 173.7 centimeters ± 3.27 (5'7") to 164.0 centimeters ± 3.80 (5'5"). The femur in the bundle burial produced an estimated stature of 168.5 ± 3.27 (5'7"). The sample size is too small to provide a reliable indication of changes in stature through time.

Paleoepidemiology

Numerous pathological conditions were noted during the sorting and identification of the skeletal elements. Pathologies observed were healed fractures, lesions, and growth abnormalities including Harris lines and enamel hypoplasias. All bones were macroscopically inspected for pathological lesions. The highly fractured condition of the bones may have obscured some pathologies. As a whole, the sample displayed few pathologies. Only 2 percent of the individuals had infectious lesions (Marks 1991). In all cases, the presence of newly forming bone at the lesion site indicated the infection was diminishing at the time of death.

Traumatic injury, as indicated by healed fractures, was identified in only 5 percent of the population (Marks 1991). The majority of the fractures involved hand and foot bones. In one instance, the severity of the fracture left the hand in a permanently bent condition and probably rendered the digits useless. In most instances, however, the healed fractures did not appear to have impaired the use or movement of the affected limb.

Harris Lines

Harris lines, otherwise known as opaque transverse lines, are found in the cancellous portion of long bones and are believed to mark acute arrest periods during the growth and development of the individual (Dickel, Schulz, and McHenry 1984; Marks, Rose, and Buie 1988). The cause of Harris lines is not limited to any one etiology, but they have been linked to acute periods of illness or malnutrition. The duration of the stress period is believed to be short and may occur on a seasonal basis.

Roentgenic examination of long bones and long bone fragments recovered from excavation Units k–o yielded little useful information on Harris line rates because of preservation problems. The highly fractured condition of the majority of bones from all levels promoted the disintegration of the cancellous bone and its subsequent replacement with dirt. Bones exhibiting only small cracks and root etching were found to be filled with clay.

Despite the condition of the sample, a single individual was found to have multiple Harris lines (transverse lines) in the distal diaphysis of the left femur. This individual was 7–8 years old based on the size of the distal epiphysis. The distal diaphysis fragment was X-rayed and found to have multiple Harris lines (Figure 11). This bone was recovered from Unit III level 37 and is assigned to the San Geronimo Phase of the Early Archaic. This individual may not be representative of the entire population. Due to the paucity of suitable materials, no frequency of transverse lines could be determined within or between the various burial populations.

Enamel Hypoplasias

Developmental abnormalities in tooth enamel occur if the process of enamel formation (amelogenesis) is disrupted. Disruption of amelo-

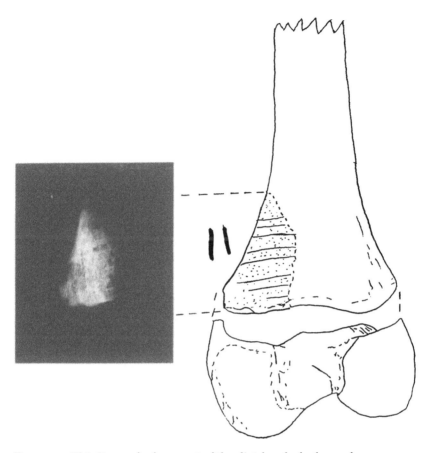

Figure 11. This X-ray of a fragment of the distal end of a femur from a 7-year-old child shows numerous opaque transverse lines or Harris lines.

genesis results in the formation of a line or series of pits in the enamel surface of the tooth crown. Although the exact factors affecting ame-logenesis have not been determined, the formation of hypoplasias is considered an excellent indicator of childhood stress episodes (Good-man, Armelagos, and Rose 1980; Rose, Condon, and Goodman 1985; Marks, Rose, and Buie 1988). The enamel on each tooth is formed during a particular stage of development. Since the developmental period is known for each tooth crown, any disturbance on that crown can be assigned a specific age. Although the exact cause of the distur-bance remains unknown, the identification of the location of hypo-plasias can determine the periods of childhood stress. Since enamel is not reworked during the lifetime of the individual, evidence of any childhood stresses that correspond with enamel formation will be contained in the adult dentition. In addition, since portions of different teeth develop at the same time, enamel defects for a particular stage of development will occur on more than one tooth. Thus, if some teeth are lost antemortem or postmortem, chances are that the remaining dentition will still have a record of any stress periods. Only in regions where severe crown attrition occurs can this information be lost.

At Bering Sinkhole, 48 percent of the San Geronimo Phase individuals have at least one hypoplasia. During the Clear Fork Phase, 45 percent of the individuals had hypoplasias and in the subsequent Round Rock and San Marcos phases, 64 percent and 66 percent of the individuals had hypoplasias, respectively. No hypoplasias were identified in either of the two partial dentitions from the Twin Sisters Phase individuals (Marks 1991). The majority of the hypoplasias occurred during the developmental periods that correspond with weaning, roughly between the ages of 2 and 5.

The observed variation in hypoplasia rates between the different cultural phase populations in the sinkhole suggests that slightly higher childhood stress occurred during the Round Rock and San Marcos phases. Similar levels of childhood stress have been identified in the Late Archaic populations of eastern Oklahoma (Marks, Rose, and Buie 1988:103). The 48 percent hypoplasia rate for the San Geronimo Phase individuals in Bering Sinkhole indicates lower childhood stress for the Edwards Plateau group than that suggested by the 100 percent hypoplasia rates for 5 Early Archaic individuals from Seminole Sink (Marks, Rose, and Buie 1988:103).

The results of the hypoplasia analysis indicate that chronic stress, in this case childhood stress, increased during the Round Rock and San Marcos phases. Unfortunately, the lack of Harris line data prevents an assessment of the relative ratio of acute stress to chronic stress for each of the cultural periods. Without this comparison, it is difficult to ascertain changes associated with different levels of stress that have been identified with changing cultural patterns, particularly subsistence shifts (Dickel, Schulz, and McHenry 1984:447).

Paleodiet

Changes in diet were determined through the analysis of dentitions and stable isotopes (Marks, Rose, and Buie 1988; Krueger and Sullivan 1984). The dentitions from the sinkhole populations were inspected for caries and microwear attributes. In addition, stable carbon and nitrogen isotope analysis was performed on the collagen and apatite fractions of arm bones.

Caries

Caries rates provide a measure of oral health and hygiene that is directly related to diet, tooth morphology, and environmental factors such as groundwater minerals. Caries are the end result of degradation of tooth surfaces due to microfloral agents. Diets high in carbohydrates are more cariogenic than are low carbohydrate diets. Thus, changes in diets can be reflected in changes in the rates of caries (Marks, Rose, and Buie 1988).

The frequencies of caries per tooth and per individual have been widely used to track changes in subsistence modes, particularly in the adoption of agriculture (Dickel, Schulz, and McHenry 1984:450; Rose et al. 1984:394). Cultigens such as corn and manioc are high in carbohydrates, and their consumption produces high caries rates. The correlation of carbohydrate consumption and high caries rates provides a relative scale for determining when a hunter-gatherer subsistence mode shifts to a horticultural pattern (Rose 1984). In areas where nondomesticates with high carbohydrate content are consumed in mass quantities, the caries rate is indistinguishable from that of the agriculturists. This was found to be the case in the lower Pecos region of Texas where the Archaic hunter-gatherers relied on succulents with a high carbohydrate content (Marks, Rose, and Buie 1988; Turpin, Henneberg, and Riskind 1986) and was also found in California where acorns became the staple food item (Dickel, Schulz, and McHenry 1984:440).

The dentitions from 35 adult individuals from all levels were used in the determination of caries per person (c/p). A rate of 1.06 c/p was obtained for the entire Archaic at Bering Sinkhole. This rate is consistent with caries rates obtained from other Archaic mortuary samples (Table 12). When the Bering sample is divided into the phases proposed by Weir (1976), a trend develops. The caries per person rate for each of the five phases is 0.69 for the San Geronimo, 0.71 for the Clear Fork, 1.62 for the Round Rock, 1.60 for the San Marcos, and 1.00 for the Twin Sisters. The caries per person rate for the Round Rock and San Marcos phases was more than double that for the preceding Clear Fork and San Geronimo phases. This suggests that a subsistence change occurred, probably reflecting the increased consumption of a high carbohydrate food. The higher caries rates are still within the range determined for Archaic hunter-gatherers in North America (Table 12) and are just below the rate of 1.8 c/p seen in the Early Archaic population from Seminole Sink. The high caries rate at Seminole Sink is attributed to the consumption of carbohydrate-rich desert succulents (Marks, Rose, and Buie 1988). The low caries rate of .69 c/p in

Table 12 *Comparison of Caries Rates from Bering Sinkhole with Caries Rates from Hunter-Gatherer and Horticulturist Sites*

Culture and Site	Caries/Person	Caries/Tooth
Archaic		
Bering Sinkhole	1.06 (35)	n.d.
Seminole Canyon	1.8 (10)	0.28 (64)
Indian Knoll	0.5 (145)	0.04 (1958)
Wister-Fourche Maline		
Mahaffey	0.1 (56)	0.04 (199)
Sam and Wann	0.8 (45)	0.08 (489)
McCutchan-McLaughlin	1.6 (24)	0.10 (385)
Bug Hill	0.2 (6)	0.01 (84)
Caddo I		
Crenshaw	5.6 (8)	0.20 (228)
Caddo II		
Belcher I	8.0 (5)	0.25 (203)
Bentsen-Clark	1.7 (31)	0.14 (383)
Ferguson	4.4 (7)	0.20 (153)
Sam Kaufman	3.0 (19)	0.16 (358)

Source: Modified from Marks et al. (1988).

the comparable Early Archaic sample from Bering Sinkhole suggests that the central Edwards Plateau groups consumed foods with a substantially lower carbohydrate content. The dearth of Middle Archaic burials from the lower Pecos region precludes comparison of rates during the Round Rock Phase of the Bering Sinkhole population.

Caries rates from other regions of Texas are based on samples obtained by combining burial populations from numerous sites of different time periods and thus are not readily comparable to the stratified Bering populations. For example, in the lower Pecos region, the Late Archaic burial population was combined with the Early Archaic Seminole Sink population to produce a rate of 1.13 c/p ($n = 52$) for the entire Archaic (Hartnady and Rose 1991:271). Since the Early Archaic rate for Seminole Sink is known to be 1.8 c/p ($n = 10$), an average rate of 0.95 c/p is estimated for the 42 lower Pecos individuals of primarily Late Archaic age. The estimated 0.95 c/p for the Late Archaic population in the lower Pecos compares favorably to the Late Archaic San Marcos Phase rate of 1.00 c/p from Bering Sinkhole, suggesting a similar carbohydrate content diet in both regions during this time.

The stratified burial population at the Ernest Witte site on the Gulf

Table 13 *Number of Adults with Caries/Total Number of Adults*

	Bering Sinkhole		Ernest Witte		Loma Sandia	
San Marcos	2/3	0.67	28/110	0.26	23/121	0.19
Round Rock	24/6	0.67	5/39	0.13		
Clear Fork	4/6	0.67				
San Geronimo	5/9	0.56				
Total	15/24					

Coastal Plain yielded caries rates (expressed as percentage of adults with caries) significantly below the same rates for the Bering Sinkhole populations of similar age (Table 13). Only 13 percent of the Ernest Witte Middle Archaic individuals had at least one caries compared to 67 percent of the Middle Archaic Round Rock Phase Bering Sinkhole sample. Likewise, the Late Archaic Ernest Witte rate of 26 percent falls far below the San Marcos Bering Sinkhole rate of 67 percent, although this difference could be exaggerated by the small sample size of the Bering Sinkhole San Marcos Phase adult population ($n = 3$).

Unfortunately, the only caries information from the Loma Sandia site is not expressed in a form comparable to Bering Sinkhole or Ernest Witte. A total of 23 teeth from a sample of 1,103 teeth were found to have caries. If each carious tooth came from a separate individual, then the percentage of individuals with at least one cavity would be approximately 19 percent (based on a sample size of 121 individuals) (Shoup 1985). This rate falls midway between the Middle and Late Archaic rates at Ernest Witte and reflects a diet more similar to the Ernest Witte population than to that at Bering Sinkhole.

The increase in caries is interpreted to indicate a shift in subsistence practices from a generalized foraging pattern to a collecting mode relying on a high-yield, high-carbohydrate staple during the Middle Archaic on the Edwards Plateau. This pattern is different from that identified in the adjacent lower Pecos region where a diet high in carbohydrates was consumed throughout the prehistoric sequence.

In central Texas, the shift to a high-cariogenic diet may indicate shifts in other aspects of culture such as the settlement pattern, whereas caries rates in the lower Pecos cannot be used as an indicator of changing cultural practices.

Occlusal Wear Patterns

During the past decade, researchers have conducted high-power microscopy on the occlusal surface of molars to define the masticatory wear patterns at the time of death (Perino and Bennett 1978; Gordon 1982; Rose, Marks, and Riddick 1983; Rose 1984). Changes in wear morphology have been linked to changes in diet. In areas where major dietary shifts occur at seasonal intervals, concomitant occlusal pattern shifts also occur. Thus, by defining the range of occlusal wear patterns in a mortuary population and linking them to certain seasonally available foodstuffs, the seasons of death can be approximated.

When linked to settlement pattern studies, the occlusal wear could indicate if the area had been inhabited throughout the entire year (cycle of seasons) or only during particular seasons. When viewed diachronically, changes in settlement/mobility and possibly dietary practices may be proposed.

The analysis of 26 molars from 24 individuals for the 7600 to 2000 B.P. burial levels at Bering Sinkhole has identified three dominant occlusal wear attributes: compression fractures, striations, and polish. These three attributes have been identified in other studies on molars from various Archaic populations where dietary components have been determined (Perino and Bennett 1978; Rose, Marks, and Riddick 1983; Rose 1984; Marks, Rose,and Buie 1988:111).

Compression fracture or pitting has been linked to the consumption of hard-shelled nuts such as hickory and pecan or pitted fruits such as chokecherry (Marks, Rose, and Buie 1988:111) where shell and pit fragments were not completely removed prior to consumption. Nut remains such as walnut, hickory, and pecan have been recovered from sites in the Edwards Plateau region (Crane 1982). Striations are attributed to the presence of grit from either grinding stones or soil contamination (Rose, Marks, and Riddick 1983). Polish is formed by a diet high in plant fiber.

The wear attributes form two patterns. The first is composed primarily of compression fractures with striations and gouges (Figure 12a). The second consists of highly polished surfaces with minute striations (Figure 12b). These patterns mirror those defined at Seminole Sink in the lower Pecos region (Marks, Rose, and Buie 1988) and at Mahaffey and Bug Hill in eastern Oklahoma (Rose, Marks, and Riddick 1983). For determining the seasonality of death, the compression fracture attribute, aligned with hardwood nut (hickory nut) consumption, suggests death during fall/winter. Polish and smoothing are subsequently aligned with spring and summer when subsistence concentrated on a high-fiber diet that included prickly pear, lechuguilla, and sotol. Striations present a kind of background noise and appear in conjunction with both pitting and polishing. Thus, the molar wear can be divided into at least two seasons, fall/winter and spring/summer, each identified by distinct dominant wear patterns.

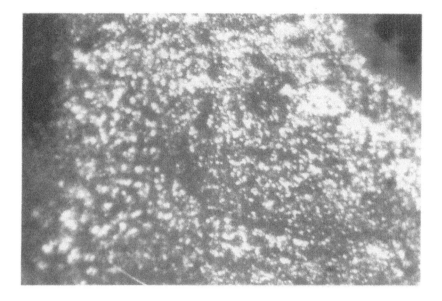

a

b

Figure 12. Photomicrographs of occlusal wear patterns on molars:
a, compression fractures, gouges, and striations (400×); b, polish and faint
striations (400×).

Table 14 *Distribution of Occlusal Wear Types by Analysis Level in Bering Sinkhole*

Level	Polish	Compression Fracture
22	2	3
23	1	0
24	3	2
25	1	0
26	0	2 (three teeth)
27	0	1
28	0	1
30	0	1
32/33	0	2
34/35	0	2
39	1	1 (two teeth)
40/41	0	1

Out of 26 molars analyzed, 18 displayed compression fractures, and 8 had polished occlusal surfaces. The small number of polished teeth gains importance when their stratigraphic context is considered (Table 14).

Pitted teeth occur throughout the stratigraphic sequence of the sample. Polished teeth, however, are predominantly found in the upper, post-3400 B.P., levels, and equal the number of pitted molars in these same levels (Table 14). The single polished tooth from level 39 indicates that this wear type also occurred in pre-3400 B.P. times. If the difference in wear patterns is related to seasonally available foodstuffs, then the pre-3400 B.P. levels reflect the dominant consumption of a single suite of foods aligned with fall/winter occupation of the area. The post-3400 B.P. dentition is equally divided between fall/winter and spring/summer wear patterns. Thus, a dual season, possibly yearlong, utilization of the area about the sinkhole is postulated in post-3400 B.P. times as opposed to a primarily single season occupation in pre-3400 B.P. times. It would not be surprising to find other seasonal wear patterns in the San Geronimo Phase dentitions because of the recovery of secondary burials that could be the remains of individuals who died during other seasons of the year when the group was not living in the sinkhole area.

Stable Carbon and Nitrogen Isotope Analysis

In recent decades, stable carbon and nitrogen isotope levels in bone and other tissues have been used to reconstruct the diet of prehistoric populations (Krueger and Sullivan 1984; Boutton et al. 1984). Plants are the base food source in the animal kingdom, and, regardless of the position in the food chain, all animals including humans eat plants or other animals that eat plants. Carbon enters the food chain through plants that obtain it from the atmosphere by the process of photosynthesis. Two photosynthetic pathways have been described for the process of reducing atmospheric CO_2 to organic carbon compounds. Most plants use the Calvin-Benson (C-3) pathway that produces a 3C compound (Boutton et al. 1984). Other plants produce a 4C compound through the Hatch-Slack (C-4) pathway. And a third group of plants (CAM) has the ability to shift from the Calvin-Benson pathway to the Hatch-Slack pathway in response to varying moisture conditions. Each of these plant groups fixes the 13C isotope in differing proportions relative to the PDB standard measure of 13C/12C (Boutton et al. 1984). Most C-3 plants have an average 13C content of -26.5 parts per mil in relation to the PDB standard, and C-4 plants average -12.5 parts per mil. CAM plants, since they can use either pathway, range between -26.5 parts per mil and -12.5 parts per mil (Turnlund and Johnson 1984).

C-3 plants are the most common type in the plant kingdom. C-4 plants are more restricted to species living in warm environments often under arid conditions. This group includes such cultigens as maize, sorghum, and sugarcane that were developed from xeric species and many grasses. CAM plants consist primarily of desert succulents such as cacti, yuccas, and lechuguillas.

Regardless of the photosynthetic pathway, each carbon compound produced in the plant is passed on to the next consumer up the food chain. The carbon compound changes in a predictable manner with each trophic level of the food chain. In this manner, the 13C/12C ratio found in a carnivore bone will reflect the carbon ratio of its herbivorous prey, which in turn, reflects the carbon ratio of the plants it consumes.

Stable carbon isotope studies have been particularly important in determining when prehistoric North American groups shifted from a predominantly C-3 plant and animal subsistence to C-4 plant consumption based on corn horticulture (Boutton et al. 1984).

A model has been proposed that relates the 13C/12C ratios (expressed as delta 13C) found in apatite and collagen fractions of bone to broad subsistence categories for human groups (Krueger and Sullivan 1984:219). The model predicts the ranges in delta 13C values of human bone apatite and collagen for eight diets (Figure 13): (1) C-3 plants; (2) C-3 plants and C-3 meat; (3) C-4 plants; (4) C-4 plants and C-4 meat; (5) marine only; (6) mixed, mainly maize; (7) C-3 plants and

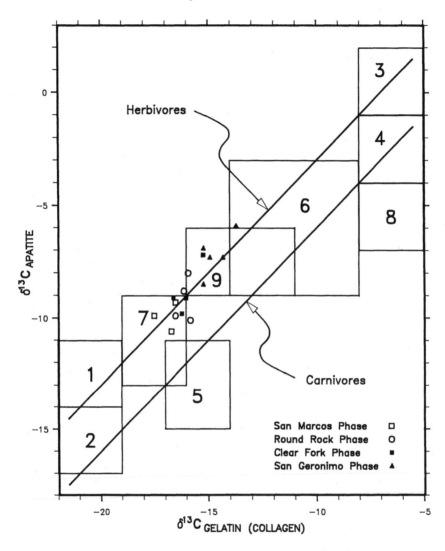

Figure 13. Plot of stable carbon and nitrogen isotope values from 16 individuals from Bering Sinkhole in relation to nine proposed dietary groups. 1, C-3 plants; 2, C-3 plants and C-3 meat; 3, C-4 plants; 4, C-4 plants and C-4 meat; 5, marine only; 6, mixed, mainly maize; 7, C-3 plants and marine; 8, C-3 plants and C-4 meat; 9, CAM plants and C-3 meat. Adapted from Krueger (1985) and Huebner (1991).

marine; and (8) C-3 plants and C-4 meat. In areas where CAM plants contribute to the diet, this model has been expanded to include a ninth diet composed of CAM plants and C-3 meat (Huebner 1991: 182). This group was defined based on isotope values obtained from Late Archaic human bone from the lower Pecos region of Texas where a diet consisting of a heavy reliance on CAM plants has been identified through coprolite and macrofossil analysis (Stock 1983). The CAM plants including yucca, lechuguilla, and prickly pear yielded delta 13C ratios averaging -13.5 parts per mil, indicating the predominant use of the C-4 pathway for photosynthesis during this time in this region.

Bering Sinkhole Stable Carbon Isotopes

A total of 16 human bone samples, representing 16 different individuals, from the stratified burial levels of Bering Sinkhole were submitted to Geochron Laboratories for stable carbon and nitrogen isotope analysis (Table 15). The analysis was sponsored by Geochron Laboratories, Cambridge, Massachusetts, as part of their Research Awards

Table 15 *Results of Stable Carbon and Nitrogen Isotope Analysis on Sixteen Individuals from Bering Sinkhole*

Lab No.	Sex	$\delta 13C$-apatite	$\delta 13C$-gelatin	$\delta 15N$-gelatin	Analysis Level
CCNR-68032	F	−10.6	−16.7	+8.1	22
CCNR-68033		−9.3	−16.5	+9.7	22
CCNR-68034	F	−9.9	−17.5	+8.2	22
CCNR-68035	M	−8.0	−15.9	+7.5	24
CCNR-68036		−8.8	−16.1	+7.1	25
CCNR-68037	M	−9.9	−16.5	+7.7	26
CCNR-68038		−10.1	−15.8	+7.8	26
CCNR-68039		−9.8	−16.2	+6.9	29
CCNR-68040	M	−9.1	−16.0	+7.3	31
CCNR-68041	M	−7.2	−15.2	+7.5	31
CCNR-68042	F	−9.1	−16.6	+8.3	31
CCNR-68043		−6.9	−15.2	+9.0	35
CCNR-68044		−8.5	−15.2	+7.4	36
CCNR-68045		−7.3	−14.3	+8.5	36
CCNR-68046	F	−7.3	−14.9	+9.6	38
CCNR-68047	M	−5.9	−13.7	+8.8	38

Program for 1991. Fifteen of the samples were from humeri, and 1 (CCNR-68036) was from a radius. All but 1 sample were from adults, and the sex of 9 of the 16 was determined by distal humerus metrics.

The cultural phases including San Geronimo, Clear Fork, Round Rock, and San Marcos were represented by sample counts of 5, 4, 4, and 3, respectively. No samples were available from the Twin Sisters Phase deposits at the time of this analysis.

The average delta 13C values of the collagen and apatite fractions for the San Geronimo, Clear Fork, Round Rock, and San Marcos populations are -14.7, -7.18; -16.0, -8.8; -16.1, -9.2; and -16.9, -9.93 parts per mil, respectively. These paired values, when plotted on a graph comparing delta 13C collagen (*x*-axis) and delta 13C apatite (*y*-axis), define a line with a slope similar to that projected for carnivores and herbivores as the diet shifts from predominantly C-3 (lower left) to predominantly CAM or C-4 (upper right). The sinkhole values over time trend toward the lower left, indicating a shift in diet away from CAM/C-4 plants and animals toward C-3 plants and animals. During the San Geronimo Phase, the diet consisted of 54.1 percent C-3 and 45.9 percent CAM/C4 foodstuffs. The Clear Fork Phase values suggest a relative increase in C-3 items to 63.7 percent of the diet and a decrease of CAM or C-4 foods to 36.3 percent. A slight increase in C-3 reliance to 64.4 percent accompanied by a CAM/C-4 decrease to 35.6 percent occurred during the Round Rock Phase. San Marcos Phase subsistence saw a marked increase in C-3 plants and animals to 70.4 percent of the diet and a decrease of CAM/C-4 items to 29.6 percent.

When the Bering Sinkhole samples are plotted in relation to the human diet models of Krueger and Sullivan (1984) and Huebner (1991), the values fall within diet groups 9 and 7 (Figure 13). Dietary group 9 consists of CAM plants and C-3 meats while group 7 consists of C-3 plants and marine foods. The decidedly inland setting of the sinkhole suggests that the group 7 diet is not applicable but that a shift in favor of C-3 foods in relation to that proposed for the group 9 diet occurred. The dearth of subsistence-related data for the area around the sinkhole precludes the identification of which C-3 plants and/or animals were emphasized during later times. It has been suggested that sotol, a C-3 diet staple in the lower Pecos area, may have expanded its range eastward across the Edwards Plateau as drying conditions during the Archaic progressed (Prewitt 1976; Wilson 1930), and pollen analysis indicates that oaks, and thus acorns, also C-3 plants, increased in number during this time (Bryant and Shafer 1977).

Stable Nitrogen Isotopes

Like carbon isotopes, nitrogen isotopes are picked up from the environment by plants. Nitrogen is obtained by plants through one of two processes: directly from the soil or through a symbiotic relationship with bacteria that draw nitrogen from the air. The majority of plants obtain nitrogen from the soil. Legumes, however, rely on nitrogen-fixing bacteria. Plants that obtain nitrogen from the soil have delta 15N values between 2 and 5 parts per mil whereas legumes average 0 parts per mil (Huebner 1991:177). With each trophic step up the food chain, nitrogen values are enriched by approximately 3 parts per mil. In this fashion, delta 15N values of a herbivore are 3 parts per mil higher than the plants consumed, and a carnivore is enriched by an additional 3 parts per mil for a total value that is 6 parts per mil higher than the plants at the base of the food chain (Schoeninger and DeNiro 1984).

Nitrogen ratios also vary according to soil conditions. Plants adapted to saline or arid soils tend to have higher nitrogen values than plants in mesic settings (Heaton 1987). Due to this variation, nitrogen analysis can also provide information concerning paleoenvironmental reconstructions.

Nitrogen isotope analyses have the potential to distinguish between leguminous and nonleguminous diets, suggest the ratio of meat-to-plant consumption, and provide data concerning paleoenvironmental reconstruction. Stable nitrogen isotope analysis was conducted on human materials from Bering Sinkhole to provide a measure of meat-to-plant consumption ratio and possibly add to the paleoenvironmental reconstruction.

Stable nitrogen isotope analysis was conducted on the collagen fraction of the same 16 human bones used in the stable carbon isotope analysis. The samples produced values ranging from 6.9 to 9.7 parts per mil with an overall average of 8.1 parts per mil (Table 15). When segregated into cultural periods, the average values for the San Geronimo, Clear Fork, Round Rock, and San Marcos phases are 8.7, 7.5, 7.5, and 8.7 parts per mil, respectively. These results can be interpreted in a number of ways, but until in depth subsistence data is obtained for this area of Texas, any interpretation should be treated as speculation. With this caveat in mind, the relatively low values of delta 15N suggest these hunter-gatherers consumed more plant foods than meat, especially during the Clear Fork and Round Rock phases. That the differences observed could be related to changing environmental conditions seems unlikely, since the pollen and faunal records for the region suggest a trend to aridity from the San Geronimo through the Round Rock phases followed by an increase in moisture during the San Marcos (Bryant and Shafer 1977). Following the environmental model, nitrogen values should increase steadily from San Geronimo through Round Rock times and then decrease during the wetter San Marcos Phase. The stable nitrogen isotope study of Bering Sinkhole human remains is not refined enough to provide detailed environmental data.

Summary of Isotope Analyses

The stable carbon and nitrogen isotope analyses of 16 individuals representing four of the five Archaic phases in Bering Sinkhole indicate that qualitative shifts in the diet occurred through time. If CAM plants employed a C-4 pathway during the Archaic period as indicated in other studies (Huebner 1991), then the Bering Sinkhole populations shifted from a diet composed of 54 percent C-3 plants/ animals and 45 percent CAM/C-4 plants/animals during the San Geronimo to a dietary ratio of 64 percent C-3 and 36 percent CAM/C-4 for the Clear Fork and Round Rock phases. The diet continued the trend toward C-3 plants and animals during the San Marcos with a 70 percent reliance on C-3 plants/animals over a 30 percent CAM/C-4 component. Although not conclusive, the stable nitrogen isotope analysis suggests that plants contributed a higher percentage of the diet than did meat during all four periods.

Grooved and Abraded Tooth Surfaces

Interproximal grooves have been identified on New World dentitions ranging in age from 7000 B.P. to the historic period (Ubelaker, Phenice, and Bass 1969:145). Proposed causes of the grooves include the use of cylindrical tooth probes, flexible palliative instruments, grit-laden salivary hydraulics, and the processing of plant fibers.

The study of the dentition from the sinkhole identified numerous grooved and abraded teeth. A sample of 189 teeth representing an estimated 32 individuals, from burial lenses dated from 7600 to 2000 B.P., was analyzed. The dentition of individuals ranging in age from 2 years to over 50 years was macroscopically and microscopically viewed for evidence of grooving. Initially, the dentition of each individual was viewed under a 10× power microscope to determine the presence or absence of grooving. All teeth were analyzed. The presence of a single tooth with grooves was sufficient for a positive rating of the dentition. However, for a negative rating, at least 4 teeth from the same individual had to be devoid of grooving. While this does not guarantee the absence of grooving on all teeth for that individual, it does provide a minimum standard. The highly fractured and dispersed condition of the sample precluded the recovery of all teeth within the dentition of each individual. In addition, the high postmortem loss of teeth further limited the number of teeth per individual available for study.

Once grooves had been identified, these teeth were viewed under 160× power magnification to determine the orientation of any abrasions within the grooves. In instances where more than 1 tooth of an individual had abrasions, the dentition was viewed macroscopically to determine any bilateral patterns or alignments.

The initial low-power microscopy disqualified 3 of the 32 individuals due to an insufficient number of teeth to meet the minimum requirement for nonabraded status. No grooves were found on any of the 8 children's dentitions (deciduous or secondary dentitions) aged 2 through 7. Only 3 adult individuals were represented by 4 or more nonabraded teeth and thus were classified as nongrooved dentitions, leaving 21 adult dentitions with at least 1 grooved tooth. Four of the individuals with grooved teeth were represented by only 1 tooth. These individuals could not be used in determining groove alignments; however, they were included in the tally of grooved teeth by tooth type.

The remaining 17 individuals had sufficiently complete dentitions to indicate patterning in the location and orientation of the grooves. Groove locations were interproximal, occlusal, lingual, and labial/buccal. In many instances, a single individual exhibited grooves in all four locations.

Grooved dentitions were found in males and females. Burials from all time periods from 7600 to 2000 B.P. displayed grooved and abraded teeth. Grooves were found on examples of all surfaces above the gum line and on all teeth of the mandible and maxillary except the M3s, right maxillary P2, right maxillary I1, left maxillary P1, and left maxillary P2 (Table 16).

High-powered microscopy revealed minute striations that paralleled the gum line or, in the case of occlusal grooving, were oriented lingually/labially. The interproximal grooves range from cylindrical, 2-millimeter-diameter grooves to broad, 9 millimeters wide, abraded surfaces. Lingual and buccal grooves were likewise broad, abraded surfaces.

The following descriptions of a 7,500-year-old female mandibular dentition and 3,000-year-old female mandible and partial maxilla dentition illustrate the extensiveness and orientational data that suggest

Table 16 *Number of Teeth and Grooved Teeth by Tooth Type*

Tooth Type	Right Mandibular		Left Mandibular		Right Maxillary		Left Maxillary	
	No.	Grooved	No.	Grooved	No.	Grooved	No.	Grooved
I1	8	6	5	2	2	0	2	0
I2	8	4	6	4	4	2	3	1
C	5	3	5	2	4	2	6	1
P1	3	2	7	4	4	2	2	0
P2	4	3	9	6	3	0	3	0
M1	5	1	5	2	9	3	3	1
M2	5	4	8	3	5	1	5	2
M3	4	0	2	0	4	0	2	0

these grooves and abrasions were the result of repeated processing of an unknown, although postulated, plant material.

7500 B.P. Dentition

This female is represented by a near-complete mandible (Figure 14). The dental arcade has suffered the antemortem loss of both M3s with complete alveolar resorption and has partial absorption after the loss of the right M1. All other teeth are in place. No caries or calculus deposits were evident on any of the teeth; however, limited abscessing was noted at the roots of the left M1.

The occlusal wear pattern is characterized by the removal of all enamel except for a rim around the exposed dentine. The enamel rim is intact on the right P2, P1, I1, left I1, I2, C, P1, P2, and M2. The right M2 is missing the enamel on the posterior edge; the right C, on the proximal edge; the right I1, on the distal edge; and the right I2 and M2 are completely devoid of enamel. The differential hardness of the dentine and enamel resulted in a cupped occlusal surface. The left M1, although devoid of enamel, has raised anterior and posterior margins; the lingual and labial margins are rounded.

Facets, worn into the interproximal, posterior, and occlusal surfaces of many of the teeth, are the dominant characteristic of this arcade. Grooved facets are located on the lingual surfaces of the right M2, P2, P1, C, I2, I1, left I1, I2, C, P1, P2, and M2; the occlusal surface of the right M2, left M1, right C, I2, I1, left I1, and C; and interproximal grooves are found on the right P2, C, I2, I1, left I1, I2, P2, and M2 (Figure 14).

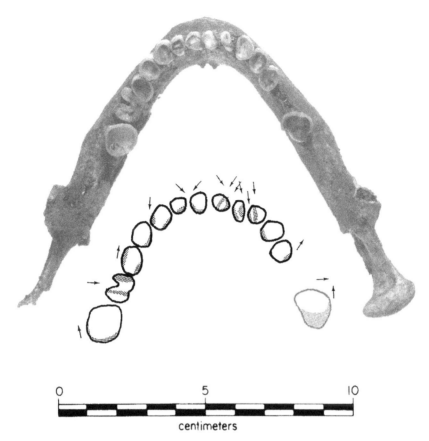

Figure 14. Photograph and line drawing of the 7,500-year-old mandible of a female. Stippled areas indicate locations of grooved or abraded surfaces. Arrows indicate possible entrance and exit loci for fibers that may have produced the grooves.

High-power microscopy indicates the grooves were worn by motion paralleling the gum line: probably the result of drawing a fiber or sinew along the teeth with sufficient force over the life of the individual to incise the enamel and dentine.

Assuming that strands were processed, each end of the strand would protrude from the mouth, thus both entry and exit loci could be identified along the dentition. The positioning and angle of the grooves identify ten interproximal entry points and six exit loci. The heavily worn right I2 was the primary entry locus; facet orientation across this tooth and the proximal and distal surfaces of adjacent teeth indicate that all six exit loci could have been utilized (accessed) from this area.

3000 B.P. Dentition

This female is represented by a right maxilla fragment with right M1, P1, C, I2 and a mandibular fragment with right M3, P2 root, C, I1, left I2, C, P1, and P2. The mandibular right M2, M1, left I1, M1, M2, and M3 were lost before death, and the right P1 and I2 were lost afterward. The condition of the maxillary fragment suggests the right M3, M2, P2, and I1 were lost prior to death. All of the left maxillary arcade is missing. Of the 4 teeth remaining in the right maxilla, the I2 and M1 have one caries each, and the C is abscessed at the root.

The upper right M1 has moved anteriorly until it is fully occluded with the P1, the P2 aveola having been resorbed. The cause of the anterior movement is attributed to fiber processing, where the fiber was passed along the posterior surface of the tooth with sufficient force to reposition the tooth and slant the occlusal surface toward the P1. The distal half of the M1 was lost in life, and the remaining portion is heavily polished and grooved—the tooth is all but extracted from the bone. All maxillary teeth have either posterior, interproximal, or occlusal grooves.

In the mandible, only the right M3 is carious, and it has two such lesions. All other teeth have posterior grooves, and the left P2, right I1, and C have interproximal grooves. The right C and P2 also have occlusal grooving. All left teeth have heavy calculus deposits anteriorly as well as posteriorly.

In the case of the left I2 and C, the calculus overlies grooving and then is subsequently grooved, suggesting that these teeth cycled through use, disuse, and back into use in processing fibers.

Discussion

For the study of grooved dentitions, new causes are proposed as new examples are analyzed. Ubelaker, Phenice, and Bass (1969), in introducing this type of study, attributed interproximal grooves to the use of predominantly stiff dental probes, although flexible probes are also suggested. Berryman, Owsley, and Henderson (1979) attribute the interproximal grooves on protohistoric Arikara dentitions to dental probes in conjunction with dietary grit. They, like Ubelaker, Phenice, and Bass (1969), associate the grooving with a palliative motive to help alleviate the discomfort of caries or aveolar resorption and further identify the practice as a male activity.

Schulz (1977), in studying 100 B.C. through A.D. 1200 Berkeley and Augustine pattern fishing village dentitions from California, identified occlusal as well as interproximal grooving on anterior teeth. In some instances, the grooves were bilaterally aligned, which prompted Schulz to conclude that the grooving in the California population was caused by the processing of plants. This was based on an ethnographic description of northern California Indians preparing fibers by pulling plant material across the occlusal surface of their teeth. Similar attributes were identified on the dentitions of Australian Aborigines, but the material processed was sinew. Again, ethnographic observation was cited in determining the material being processed (Brown and Molnar 1990).

The present study of central Texas Archaic dentitions expands the location of grooves to include labial and lingual surfaces in addition to interproximal and occlusal areas. A multitude of alignments lends further support to the inference that these grooves are the result of processing a fibrous material by pulling it across various tooth surfaces along the maxillary and mandibular dentitions.

The central Texas dentitions have grooves and abraded surfaces that range from 2 millimeters to 9 millimeters in width. The range in size possibly results from processing various sizes of plant fibers: thin strands for twine and broad strands for weaving. The commonality of grooved dentitions from all burial levels, dated between 7600 and 2000 B.P., indicates that similar processing of plant materials persisted throughout the entire Archaic period.

9. Summary and Conclusions

Summary of the Bering Sinkhole Analyses

Bering Sinkhole is a natural cavern in the Cretaceous limestone of the Edwards Plateau in central Texas. Access into the cavern is limited to a precipitous drop through a hole in the ceiling at the south end of the cavern chamber. Beginning approximately 7,500 years ago, the hunter-gatherer inhabitants of the area dropped or lowered their dead through the opening and left the bodies exposed, or partially buried under rock thrown in afterward, on a debris cone surface initially over 6 meters below the sinkhole entrance. Natural deposition, and the repeated use of the site in the disposal of the dead for at least 5,500 years, eventually filled the cavern to within 3 meters of the surface entrance. Excavations to date of the stratified deposits of the debris cone have recovered the partial remains of at least 62 individuals, representing all age groups and both sexes. The majority of the individuals had been buried as fully fleshed corpses. Also included are the remains of at least 6 cremations and 1 bundle burial. Approximately 50 percent of the debris cone and 15 percent of the deposits adjacent to the cone have been removed.

The 5,500-year span of human burial deposits reflects portions of all five Archaic phases defined by Weir (1976) for the central Texas cultural region. Bering Sinkhole provides the opportunity to compare biological and ritual aspects of Archaic cultures to the culture systems model developed by Weir.

Bering Sinkhole is not close to any of the habitation sites in the area. The nearest known habitation site is .75 kilometer south of the sinkhole, and a larger site complex of multiple large burned rock middens is located approximately 2.1 kilometers from the sinkhole. Neither site has received archaeological investigation, although the larger site has produced artifacts representing Late Paleoindian through Late Prehistoric time periods. Lithic debitage and worked cobbles, the result of lithic procurement of the fine-grained cherts that outcrop on the hill slopes, are scattered across the hill slopes and interfluves near the sinkhole.

The excavated materials from Bering Sinkhole were analyzed using a multidisciplinary approach combining site formation analysis, faunal analysis, taphonomy, material culture analysis, and human remains analysis toward the goal of macrotemporal characterization of cultures and the identification of long-term shifts in cultural systems in central Texas.

The results of the faunal analysis bolster and somewhat refine the model of Holocene paleoenvironmental reconstruction that proposes a general drying trend beginning over 7,000 years ago and continuing throughout the Holocene, interrupted approximately 2,500 years ago by a mesic period. The remains of desert cottontail and Florida cottontail rabbits from deposits dating to most of the Holocene—except the period from 2,500 to 1,500 years ago, when only the remains of the more mesic-adapted Florida cottontail were found—suggest that the xeric conditions had ameliorated during this time. That a period of heightened xeric conditions occurred just prior to 3000 B.P. is suggested by the recovery of the terrestrial snail *Glyphyalinia umbilicata* in deposits before 3400 B.P. and after 2500 B.P.

Accompanying the drying trend was a decline in soil depth and conditions. By 4500 B.P., the deep sandy soil-adapted gopher *Geomys* was replaced by *Pappogeomys*, which inhabits shallower soils. And even this gopher disappeared by 3100 B.P. leaving only *Thomomys*, which inhabits shallow rocky soils.

Material culture analysis involved artifacts made of stone, bone, antler, turtle, freshwater shell, and marine shell. All of the lithic artifacts conformed to classes previously defined in the central Texas region. Projectile point types were Martindale, Uvalde, Travis, Bulverde, and Frio, representing only a fraction of the number of types defined for the Archaic of central Texas. Although projectile points were not very numerous in the sinkhole (*n* = 10), their distribution provided very limited insight into the seriation of some types that often co-occur in habitation sites. In this regard, the two Martindale points were found in deposits below the single Uvalde point. These two types of points are often found side by side in the same strata in habitation sites. The situation at the sinkhole suggests that Martindale dart points may predate Uvalde points in at least this area of central Texas, although the extremely small sample size may be misleading.

Travis dart points, often accompanied by Nolan points in habitation sites, were the only projectile point type from the Clear Fork Phase in the sinkhole. In this instance, of course, the sinkhole data cannot suggest—in the absence of Nolan points—whether Travis predated Nolan, but rather that the two types do not always co-occur in central Texas. The distribution of Bulverde and Frio dart points support the sequence proposed for central Texas (Weir 1976).

With the exception of the cache of large bifaces and a drill, the remaining lithic artifacts, composed of unifaces, bifaces, hammerstones, and cores, are not noteworthy in a utilitarian sense; however, their presence in a burial context is significant in characterizing the burial programs. This is discussed later. The cache of 14 large, early stage bifaces and 1 drill is significant in a number of ways. Through statistical analysis of technological and idiosyncratic attributes, it was determined that at least 3 flintknappers were responsible for the manufacture of the bifaces. Such group investment in burial offerings suggests the high-quality cherts and fine workmanship were of economic and ritual importance. Further support of this is found in the archaeological record in areas south and east of the Edwards Plateau, where biface blanks of Edwards chert have been recovered. These bifaces were traded to chert-poor areas. The recovery of a number of biface caches from Loma Sandia on the Gulf Coastal Plain provides further evidence that Edwards cherts were important trade items.

Bone artifacts were awls, pins, engraved implements, and tubular beads. The awls and pins were made from deer bone, and deer-sized bone was used to make the incised bone implements. The beads were made from rabbit and turkey long bones, and a single bone bangle was made from a badger leg bone. The awls were apparently utilitarian items, whereas the pins and beads were articles of personal adornment. The engraved bone implements are similar to specimens found in burial contexts in areas east of the Edwards Plateau (Hall 1981, n.d.). Hall (1988:170) has proposed that the design elements on bone batons or pointed implements are group signifiers, and, through intersite comparisons of designs, he postulates that area-specific designs could be identified. The zigzag line and short bar design on the sinkhole specimens are different from the designs found at other sites discussed by Hall. Whether this design is individual-specific, site-specific, or area-specific cannot be determined at the present time. The sinkhole specimens predate the implements discussed by Hall (1988) by approximately 500 years. Those discussed by Hall (1988) are Late Archaic or San Marcos–equivalent age, while the sinkhole implements belong to the terminal Round Rock Phase.

Antler artifacts consist of one antler billet used in the reduction of lithic tools and numerous antler tines, antler fragments, and beams still attached to the animal's skull cap. The numerous fragments un-

doubtedly represent complete antler racks that have partially disinte-
grated in the damp sinkhole conditions. Some of the fragments are
badly burned. Deer antler racks have been recovered from burial contexts in the large burial sites of southeast Texas and smaller sites or
individual interments along the Balcones Escarpment (Bement 1987;
Hall 1981; Lukowski 1988; Taylor and Highley n.d.). In most instances, numerous racks, sometimes still attached to the skull, were
laid directly on top of the corpse in the burial sequence. Burned antler
is also common in these instances. With the exception of cases where
the antler is worked into a specific tool, antlers recovered from burial
contexts are best explained as the result of ritual activity.

A single artifact of turtle carapace was recovered from the sinkhole.
This implement may have been a bowl or hair ornament or may have
served as both. Turtle shell containers have been found in burial contexts at Horn Shelter (Young 1985:39). There, 5 carapace bowls were
found in various associations with the burials. Three of the carapace
artifacts were stacked and placed under the head. The Horn Shelter
specimens are dated to the Late Paleoindian period. At Bering Sinkhole, the carapace artifact was recovered from the San Geronimo
Phase burials. The hypothesis that the Bering specimen served as a
hair ornament stems from the recovery of a long, slender bone pin
from directly under the smashed carapace. The bone pin was of sufficient length and thinness to pass between the narrow gaps in the
costal plates of the carapace. In such a position, the pin and the carapace could have functioned as a barrette or hair ornament. The removal of the vertebral arches from the inside of the carapace is consistent with alteration necessary for the artifact to function as a bowl.

Unaltered freshwater mussel shell valves have been recovered from
burial contexts of various ages (Turpin 1992; Taylor and Highley n.d.).
The function of the shell halves is not known, although it has been
hypothesized that they served as containers, plates, or spoons.

Marine shell ornaments have drawn considerable attention in
North American archaeology. This attention stems from the recovery
of numerous large shell pendants from burial contexts across the
southeastern United States, along the Mississippi River drainage system, and in southeast Texas. The Texas sample alone contained exotic
artifacts from as far away as Arkansas and possibly Florida (Hall
1981:303). The pendants, made of conch shell, may have come from
the Florida rather than the Texas coast (Hall 1981:295). However, the
origin of these objects remains to be demonstrated. The 2 conch shell
pendants from Bering Sinkhole were recovered from the Early Archaic San Geronimo Phase deposits. One is made from the outside
whorl of the conch, and its form is identical to ones recovered from

Late Archaic contexts in southeast Texas (Hall 1981). The second pendant is made from the columella of the conch. Columella pendants are also common during the Late Archaic of southeast Texas; however, the form of the Bering pendant is unlike any recovered from Late Archaic contexts. The Bering pendant required that the columella be trimmed to a rectangular tablet rather than its original cylindrical form. The significance of the Bering conch pendants lies in the considerable age of the technology used in fashioning such items that until now has been attributed solely to Late Archaic peoples.

Small marine shell beads are relatively rare in assemblages from Texas, although when found they are usually from burial contexts (Hall 1981). Their relative rarity is probably a function of their small size. That more are found in burial contexts is probably attributable to the special recovery techniques often employed by archaeologists in burial fill analysis.

The material culture recovered from the sinkhole is a mixture of utilitarian, personal adornment, trade, and ritual items. The sinkhole has provided new data concerning the possible age and function of some of the artifacts that have wide distributions in Texas.

Analysis of the human skeletal remains included consideration of taphonomy, paleodemography, paleoepidemiology, and paleodiet with the goal of reconstructing the biological aspects of the populations living in this area of the Edwards Plateau. The skeletal remains provided the means of identifying the various strata of sinkhole use through the plotting of long bones that allowed the projection of depositional surfaces across the borders of individual excavation units. While the wet conditions of the sinkhole deposits preserved some aspects of bone morphology, the destructive forces of gravity, animal gnawing, and water transport disarticulated and dispersed the skeletal elements to such a degree that it was impossible to reconstruct individual skeletons. The dispersed and intermingled condition hampered age and sex determinations that rely on the use of different bone and tooth attributes from the same individual to produce reliable results.

A minimum number of 62 individuals of both sexes and all agegroups were recovered from the sinkhole deposits. The presence of both sexes and all age-groups in the various deposits indicate that the burial facility was available to all members of the society and not limited to a certain segment. The egalitarian nature of the mortuary facility is consistent with the societal reconstruction of central Texas hunter-gatherer groups determined by site and tool assemblage analysis (Weir 1976:140).

Through the identification of pathologies attributed to disease and nutritional stress, it was learned that the archaic hunter-gatherers in this area of the Edwards Plateau were healthy, robust, and virtually free of acute pathologies. Infections were identified on only 2 percent of the individuals and in these instances were accompanied by re-modeled bone, suggesting that the infections were subsiding. Trau-matic injury occurred in 5 percent of the individuals and consisted mainly of broken hand and foot bones. Again, all traumas had healed. Acute and chronic nutritional stress indicators included Har-ris lines in long bones and enamel hypoplasias of the teeth. Due to the highly fractured condition of the long bones, it was impossible to establish an occurrence rate of Harris lines. In fact, only one case of Harris lines was identified in the long bone of a 7-year-old in the San Geronimo Phase burial sample.

Teeth were well represented in the various burial zones but often as loose isolates. In this instance, however, enough associated denti-tions were available from each burial zone to establish hypoplasia rates. During the San Geronimo Phase, 48 percent of the individuals had enamel hypoplasias. Only 45 percent of the Clear Fork individ-uals had hypoplasias. Round Rock and San Marcos phase burials had hypoplasia rates of 64 and 66 percent, respectively. No hypoplasias were found in either of the 2 Twin Sisters Phase individuals. In all instances, hypoplasias corresponding to the developmental age range often associated with weaning (2–4 years old) were the most com-mon. Interestingly, most individuals with hypoplasias during the 4-to-6-year range died between the ages of 7 and 12 years.

The increase in hypoplasia rates, although not substantial, mirrors a similar increase seen in caries rates. During the San Geronimo Phase, the caries rate was .69 caries per person (c/p). A similar rate of 0.71 c/p was found for the Clear Fork Phase. The caries rate in-creased at least twofold to a level of 1.62 c/p during the Round Rock Phase and 1.60 c/p for the San Marcos Phase and then dropped slightly to 1.00 c/p during the Twin Sisters Phase. These values fall in the upper range of caries rates described for Archaic hunter-gatherers across North America, yet are well below that experienced by horti-cultural groups. The comparison of the sinkhole caries rate of 0.69 c/p of San Geronimo age with the rate of 1.8 c/p from comparable Early Archaic burials from the neighboring lower Pecos region indicates that substantially different diets were consumed in the two regions. If the amount of carbohydrates in the diet is indeed a primary factor in caries rates, as suggested by numerous researchers (Marks, Rose, and Buie 1988; Hartnady and Rose 1991), then the central Texas

groups near the sinkhole did not have a diet of comparable carbohydrate content to that of the lower Pecos inhabitants until the Round
Rock Phase, approximately 1,000 years later.

The study of stable carbon and nitrogen isotopes of 16 individuals
from San Geronimo through San Marcos age deposits in the sinkhole
indicate that the diet shifted from a 54.1 percent reliance on C-3 plants
and animals during the San Geronimo Phase to a 70.4 percent reliance
on C-3 plants and animals during the San Marcos Phase. Diets during
the intervening phases consisted of 63.7 percent C-3 plants and animals during the Clear Fork Phase and 64.4 percent C-3 reliance during the Round Rock Phase. The stable nitrogen isotope analysis suggests that plant foodstuffs consistently dominated animals in the diet
throughout the Archaic in this portion of the Edwards Plateau. The
steady increase in consumption of C-3 plants over CAM/C-4 plants
and the increase in caries rates suggest that a high-carbohydrate C-3
plant or suite of plants became increasingly important in the diet
through time.

Occlusal wear patterns of the molars indicate that at least two dominant wear types were present throughout the Archaic. Pitted, rough
occlusal surfaces formed the dominant wear pattern throughout the
Archaic. This wear pattern is consistent with the consumption of
plant foods that contain a hard component such as nut shells or fruit
pits (Marks, Rose, and Buie 1988). The second most common pattern
consisted of smooth, highly polished surfaces. This wear pattern is
consistent with the consumption of a high-fiber diet, particularly including desert succulents (Marks, Rose, and Buie 1988). The distinct
occurrence of one wear type to the almost exclusion of the other on
the dentitions from a single individual suggests that each wear is the
product of a seasonally distinct foodstuff. Although this has not been
substantiated in Texas, the pitted wear pattern is proposed to represent a fall/winter or winter/early spring diet of nuts, and the polished
wear is aligned with a late spring/summer diet of high-fiber foods
(Marks, Rose, and Buie 1988).

The distribution of these two primary wear patterns in the sinkhole
suggests that the San Geronimo and Clear Fork burials are dominated
by fall/winter burials and that the subsequent Round Rock and San
Marcos burials represent an even distribution between fall/winter and
spring/summer burials. The implications for the different seasonal
use of the sinkhole and the relationship between settlement patterns
and sinkhole use are significant and will be discussed further in the
following sections.

A final finding of the bioarchaeological analysis was the identification of numerous interproximal grooves and abraded surfaces at the

cemento-enamel junction on numerous teeth in the maxilla and mandible from individuals of all time periods. Interproximal grooving is purported to be the result of one of a number of ways where either plant or sinew strands are processed in the mouth by pulling the fibers across or through the dentitions or where pointed wooden instruments are used as tooth picks to remove food from between the teeth. The symmetrical alignments of the grooves and abraded surfaces found on the Bering Sinkhole specimens suggest that plant or sinew processing is responsible. That these similar grooves are found in the adult dentitions from the burial levels in San Geronimo, Clear Fork, Round Rock, and San Marcos phases suggests that a similar processing of materials, probably for a similar purpose, was conducted throughout the Archaic in this area of the Edwards Plateau. None of the Twin Sisters Phase dentitions were available at the time of this study. Dentitions of adults of both sexes contain these grooves. Although the exact material being processed cannot be identified, similar grooves have been produced in the dentitions of ethnographic California groups processing plant fibers for basketry and twining and of ethnographic Australian groups processing sinew for use in tying objects together (Schulz 1977; Brown and Molnar 1990).

From this summary of the results of the various analyses undertaken on Bering Sinkhole materials, it is seen that the Archaic period of the central Texas Edwards Plateau is characterized by change and not stasis. Change has been found in the faunal assemblages that have inhabited the region during the past 8,000 years. Change has been identified in the cultural aspects of hunter-gatherer groups through time, and change occurs in the biological attributes of the inhabitants during the long Archaic period. The task that remains to be completed is the correlation of the changes and attributes of the Bering Sinkhole mortuary data with the cultural reconstructions obtained through the analysis of settlement, subsistence, and material culture remains at habitation sites on the Edwards Plateau of central Texas.

Reconstructed Use of Texas Sinkholes

Previous work at sinkhole mortuary sites has resulted primarily in descriptive reports emphasizing the number of burials, associated artifacts, and age of the deposits (Benfer and Benfer 1962). Due to the highly fragmentary condition of most of the skeletal materials, both Elcor and Mason mortuary sinkholes were thought to contain secondary burials (Skinner 1978; Skinner, Haas, and Wilson 1980; Benfer and Benfer 1962). The recovery of partially articulated remains at Hitzfelder (Givens 1968) and Seminole Sink (Bement 1985b), however, suggested that postdepositional rather than cultural factors were at work in these similar sites. At Bering Sinkhole, the recovery of articulated remains, cremations, and bundles confirm that secondary as well as primary interments were placed in sinkholes. When these burial types are found in different sinkholes or at different time periods in the same sinkhole, they can be explained as evidence for the use of different burial programs by different cultural groups. However, when both secondary and primary burial modes are represented in the same deposit from a single site, their meaning must be reevaluated.

On the one hand, the theoretical perspective, that observed differences in the handling of the dead equate to the different social positions or personas of the deceased (Binford 1971), would imply that the sinkhole populations contained individuals of varied statuses. Alternately, different treatment of individuals could be determined in relation to mobility strategies and settlement scheduling (Charles and Buikstra 1983:132; Jirikowic 1990). In these cases, whether an individual was cremated, bundled, or left articulated was determined by the time and distance remaining before the next scheduled stop at the mortuary or aggregation site.

The recovery of the cremation from the top of the Seminole Sink deposits and of isolated remains from other sinkholes (Turpin and Bement 1988:10) suggests that sporadic or expediency use of sinkholes also occurred.

What then, do these various forms of sinkhole use say about cultural patterns on the Edwards Plateau? An analysis of the diachronic distribution of burials in Bering Sinkhole is conducted here to formulate a possible answer to this question.

When viewed from the perspective of Weir's (1976) cultural phases, the use of Bering Sinkhole was fairly constant with rates of .009 burials per year (b/y) during the San Geronimo Phase, .010 b/y for the Clear Fork Phase, .009 b/y for the Round Rock Phase, and .008 b/y for the San Marcos Phase. Only during the subsequent Twin Sisters Phase did the rate drop to .003 b/y. However, viewing the burial rates per year in macro time units such as phases masks differences in sinkhole use visible at finer time scales. When burial rate per year is calculated for each analysis level, using MNI and level ages computed from depositional rates (see chapter 5), subperiod patterns appear. The distribution of MNI per level defines five periods of heightened use, four periods of intermediate use, seven periods of low use, and seven periods of no use (Figure 15). The San Geronimo Phase is composed of sporadic periods of high use separated by periods of little-

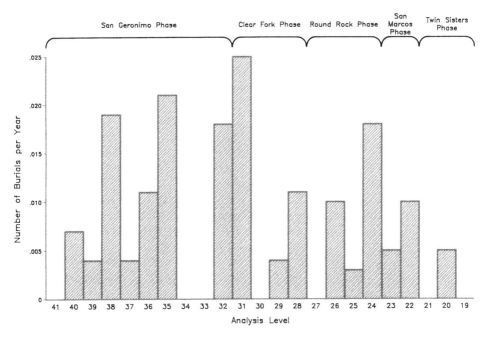

Figure 15. Bar graph of the rate of burials per year for each of the analysis levels in Bering Sinkhole.

to-no use. The Clear Fork Phase consists of one high-use period followed by no use and then a gradual increase in use. The Round Rock Phase shows varied use through time with a peak in the final centuries. San Marcos Phase use has a pattern similar to that during the Round Rock Phase, and, during the Twin Sisters Phase, the sinkhole saw sporadic use and then was abandoned. In general, the graph is characterized by two patterns (Figure 15). To the left of level 30, sinkhole use appears episodic with high peaks and low valleys. To the right of level 30, sinkhole use is more normalized, with less distance between the peaks and valleys. The extent to which sample size and the use of arbitrary analysis levels biases this graph cannot be determined until a larger area of the site is excavated. However, given these limitations, the two patterns suggest different utilization of the sinkhole that may result from different burial programs.

A hypothetical burial program is suggested for each of the sinkhole use patterns. The pattern for the left (early Archaic) side of the graph could result from a burial program that is cyclical in occurrence and ossuary in form. This would be similar to that discussed by Jirikowic (1990) (see chapter 3) where communal burials consisted of everyone who died between scheduled Feasts of the Dead. The result was sites containing bundles, cremations, and articulated skeletons placed in a single burial pit. If the ceremonies took place at different sites but eventually returned to the first site, the pattern at the latter would include peaks in burial numbers separated by periods of no use. This cyclical use of burial facilities is also described by Charles and Buikstra (1983) for Archaic hunter-gatherers in the tributary valleys of the Mississippi drainage.

> . . . the very high frequency of bundle burials and disarticulated remains at sites in the tributary valleys may indicate that most deaths occurred at such a distance from the interment facility that the bodies required processing and storage at the occupied location until final burial could be completed when the seasonal round brought the group near the cemetery. (Charles and Buikstra 1983:132)

Evidence from Bering Sinkhole to support such a reconstruction for the early periods includes the presence of cremations, a bundle burial, and partially articulated remains in the levels of peak use. Additional support includes the evidence from the dentitions that these levels are dominated by wear patterns signifying a single fall/winter season of habitation of the area yet still containing burials from other seasons as well in the form of cremations and bundle burials.

The right half of the graph could result from a quasi-sedentary settlement pattern where panseasonal habitation would allow burial of the dead in the mortuary facility shortly after death rather than the stockpiling and storage of the remains. Support for this reconstruction is found in dental wear patterns that suggest multiseasonal habitation of the area, the recovery of more articulated remains including a near-complete torso and a fetus, the recovery of trade items indicative of intergroup exchange, and the rise in number of symbolic grave goods reflecting either group identity or group investment in providing the furnishings of the dead. The elaboration of ritual seen in the right half of the graph is perhaps the strongest indication that cultural change associated with mortuary practices and other aspects of the society has transpired. Many of these attributes, especially those dealing with reduced mobility, group identity, and exchange networks, are incorporated in the mortuary program identified in the sites along the main Mississippi drainage where base camp settlements with restricted territories were common (Charles and Buikstra 1983). But at Bering Sinkhole, the distinctions suggested here between various burial rates and their corresponding mortuary patterns are so affected by limited sample size as to be almost subjective. However, in the following discussions, I hope to highlight the differences between the mortuary programs as they relate to changing population and cultural structures.

Sinkhole Use and Settlement Systems

As previously stated, the sinkhole was used as a mortuary site intermittently over a 5,500-year period between 7,500 and 2,000 years ago. Sinkhole use is tied to the settlement pattern of the area, since its employment is dependent on (1) when groups occupied the vicinity and (2) when death occurred while the group was in residency. Thus, a review of the proposed settlement system models for the central Texas area should also provide a model for sinkhole use. A number of settlement models have been proposed, and many of these have been combined into more comprehensive models. For the purposes of this discussion, the settlement/subsistence aspects of Gunn's (1977) model for the central Texas Archaic will be outlined and compared to Weir's (1976) comprehensive modeling of sociopolitical structure, specialization, and spatial patterns.

Gunn's (1977:271–276) model comprises two settlement systems termed the nomadic seasonal round and transhumant seasonal activities. His model proposes that the central Texas region has vacillated between a desert Archaic adaptation and an eastern Archaic adaptation depending on climatic conditions; more xeric conditions prompted the former while mesic conditions prompted the latter. He proposes that central Texas demography and settlement patterns can be understood by modeling three processes: (1) the shift in the arid-humid boundary, (2) the nomadic adaptation of desert Archaic during arid times, and (3) the transhumant focal economy adaptation of the eastern Archaic during mesic times (Gunn 1977).

Modeling the central Texas climate has proved to be a formidable task relying on such diverse sources of data as meteorology, palynology, paleontology, sedimentology, hydrology, volcanology, and astronomy. General climate models have been presented earlier (chapter 6) and will not be repeated here except as they correlate with settlement strategies. Suffice it to say that the arid-humid dividing line has shifted both eastward and westward of the Kerr County area during the Holocene. In addition, the arid-humid boundary is species specific. For example, Hulbert (1984) places the present range boundary for *Sylvilagus audubonii* along the Balcones Escarpment well east of Kerr County. Gunn (1977), on the other hand, defines a dividing line for an undetermined faunal or floral assemblage along a 700 millimeter precipitation isohyet that currently passes through Kerr and

Gillespie counties. What has not been accomplished, but which is the goal of subsistence/settlement modeling in central Texas, is the determination of the cultural adaptational boundary for human hunter-gatherers.

The remaining two points of Gunn's proposition—nomadic and transhumant—model settlement patterns (systems) and bear on the problem of the episodic use of Bering Sinkhole. The nomadic seasonal round model, predating Binford's (1980) residential mobility model, is based on the tenets of Steward's desert Archaic subsistence pattern and expands Prewitt's (1974:1–20) model of exploitive and management systems. These models predict that human groups, organized as bands, move across the landscape to prescribed locations of known, seasonally exploitable resources. Site locations are often determined by proximity to highest valued items in areas of unequally valued resources. The resources are either "exploited" until a point of diminishing returns is reached or "managed," at which time the group moves at a time that ensures the complete and rapid rejuvenation of the resource.

> Repeated occupation of a given site is governed in theory by fore-knowledge of the location of desired resources, or in the case where different cultures have located at the same spot, resources that were coincidentally valued in all cases were available at the same place over long periods of time. (Gunn 1977:272)

Upon depletion of the resources at one site, movement of the band to another locality was based on the prior knowledge of the availability of the next scheduled resource. If, however, the next predetermined area failed to contain the anticipated resources, perhaps due to local environmental conditions (such as a hailstorm), then the band either (1) searched for a comparable new locality; (2) returned to the first site to further deplete the resources until the next scheduled resource would become available; or (3) expanded the types of resources to be exploited, thus taking in lower priority resources until the next scheduled resource would be available. These three options are not mutually exclusive, but rather a combination of them is probable.

In contrast to the nomadic seasonal round model, the transhumant model consists of a more sedentary band in which labor intensity is preferred over mobility. In this model, a labor force targets specific resources in season. A task group sets up a transhumant station where the targeted resource is stockpiled until a sufficient quantity is obtained for transport back to the band center. At the village, the produce from the various task groups is evaluated for sufficiency. If the resources are insufficient to meet the needs of the group, then an alternative system of options including trading, raiding, or migration is implemented. Compared with the nomadic system, Gunn postulates that the transhumant system will include a larger territory and will tend to have a larger population.

Implications for Sinkhole Use

In the nomadic system, a band is composed of people under a loose structure, and membership is fluid. The band will continue to target specific areas, probably reoccupying the same sites, to exploit a known seasonal resource. However, if an area fails to produce, a new area with comparable resources will be found and exploited, possibly leaving the initial area abandoned for an undeterminable period of time. Another factor that could result in the abandonment of an area is the dissolving of a band, its members joining neighboring bands that utilize different sites. In these instances, the productive resource areas utilized by the first band would remain in the collective memory of the second band only so long as the new members remained in residency. Death or subsequent migration of those members with this knowledge would remove this knowledge until such a time as the resources were rediscovered. If a sinkhole was located in an area seasonally visited by the nomadic band, its use would mirror that of the resource area. When the band dissolved or moved to other resource areas, the sinkhole would be abandoned in lieu of another sinkhole or alternative burial mode. The widespread availability of sinkholes suggests that availability of a suitable feature was not a problem. The discovery of burials in a large number of sinkholes across the Edwards Plateau lends further support to the suitability of the widespread features as burial loci. The unpredictability of death further suggests that a number of burial features could be employed through the course of a few years of seasonal rounds. In the nomadic adaptation, individual sinkholes should contain burials for a single season of the cycle. Of course, reuse of a site during more than one season of the cycle could lead to the burial of people during additional seasons.

The transhumant adaptation, termed logistic mobility by Binford (1980), has different implications for sinkhole use. The reduced mobility of the band would make a single sinkhole available to anyone who died throughout the extended seasons of occupation. Thus, individuals who died during various seasons would be buried in the same sinkhole. Accompanying the reduced mobility is a projected increase in the population in residence at the site, thus, a larger population to supply its dead to the sinkhole. Anyone who died away from the base camp would probably be transported to the group burial facility, perhaps first receiving primary burial or cremation to ease the labor of transport and subsequent burial in the sinkhole.

As previously stated, if, for some reason, resources were not sufficient to support the large band, trade relations with neighboring groups would be of the utmost importance as a buffering mechanism.

Expected Burial Population Characteristics Based on Proposed Settlement/Subsistence Organizational Models

The diachronic model proposed by Weir (1976) for the succession of cultures during the Archaic of central Texas suggests that at different times the hunter-gatherer groups did, indeed, follow settlement/subsistence modes that can be aligned with Gunn's two types.

According to Weir, during the San Geronimo Phase, groups were composed of loosely structured, small and highly mobile bands following a nonspecialized subsistence mode. This characterization places San Geronimo groups in the desert Archaic mode, termed nomadic by Gunn. The mortuary populations should consist of low numbers of individuals who died during a particular season of the year.

During the Clear Fork Phase, Weir proposes that the bands were larger, were seasonally less mobile, and had a specialized subsistence mode focused on plant processing. These attributes correspond more to Gunn's transhumant system and suggest that burial populations would represent the extended seasons of the year when the group was residing near the mortuary site.

A similar situation could be expected during the following Round Rock Phase when the cultural system consisted of macrobands with definite seasonal aggregations of long duration. The Round Rock Phase is characterized as a time of cultural coalescence (Weir 1976). Burial groups would be expected to contain burials representing all seasons of the year. This situation is similar to that proposed by Charles and Buikstra (1983) for hunter-gatherer groups along the main stem of the Middle Mississippi drainage. Qualitatively, the Round Rock Phase is distinct from the Clear Fork Phase by the apparent development of a highly structured sociopolitical system (Weir 1976:120).

The subsequent San Marcos Phase groups were relatively smaller in size and more mobile (Weir 1976). The burial populations during this period would expectedly be similar to those proposed for the Clear Fork Phase.

The Twin Sisters Phase groups are characterized as small, highly mobile bands (Weir 1976) and would be classed as nomadic hunter-gatherers following Gunn's (1977) critera. Burial populations would be small and consist primarily of individuals who died during a specific season when the group was in the vicinity of the burial facility. This pattern should be similar to that defined for the San Geronimo Phase.

The Bering Sinkhole Mortuary Pattern

The results of the analysis of the Bering Sinkhole mortuary sample deviate from the expected patterns of mortuary populations outlined above in several significant ways.

The first aspect of Gunn's model that attempts to link shifts in cultural systems with changing environmental conditions is only grossly applicable to the Bering Sinkhole data. Results of the paleontological analysis suggest that the area in the vicinity of the sinkhole became increasingly drier beginning in the San Geronimo Phase, through the Clear Fork Phase, and reached a peak of aridity during the Round Rock Phase. Conditions during the subsequent San Marcos Phase were comparatively more mesic and then returned to increased xeric tendencies during the Twin Sisters Phase.

If the cultural system could be linked to these shifts in climate, the central Texas Archaic groups should have followed a nomadic system during San Geronimo, Clear Fork, and Round Rock times; a transhumant system during the San Marcos Phase; and a return to a nomadic system during the Twin Sisters Phase. As is evident in the proposed cultural systems reconstructed by Weir (1976) using artifact and site data sets, the cultural systems do not correlate with the environmental conditions *at the level described by the paleontological and palynological analyses*. The problem with this kind of correlation, as I stated earlier, is that the adaptational shift for human cultures has not been determined in central Texas. Thus, the shifts noted in plant and animal communities may not have been of sufficient magnitude to effectively alter the human adaptational systems.

Since aspects of Weir's cultural model correspond with the settlement/subsistence aspects contained in Gunn's nomadic versus transhumant model, the latter will not be dismissed solely because of problems of correlating the environmental changes. By this same token, the reconstructed changes in climate, especially as they affected certain plant and animal species of economic importance to the human inhabitants, remain important.

Returning to the assessment of Weir's cultural model in light of the results from the mortuary sample from Bering Sinkhole, some sig-

Table 17 *Analysis Results by Cultural Division*

	San Geronimo Phase	Clear Fork Phase	Round Rock Phase	San Marcos Phase	Twin Sisters Phase
Analysis level	41–32	31–28	27–24	23–22	21–19
No. of burials	20	10	9	6	2
No. of cremations	2	1	2	1	
No. of Bundles	1				
Artifacts	2 Martindales, 1 Uvalde, 1 biface, 3 unifaces, 7 mussel shells, 1 bone awl, 1 bone pin, 2 antler fragments, 2 marine shell pendants, 1 turtle carapace bowl	3 Travis, 1 biface, 1 multicore, bone beads, 1 bone awl, 1 incised pin tip, numerous antler frags., 1 mussel shell	1 Bulverde, 1 burned point, biface cache, incised bone, 1 biface, unicore, incised bone implements, bone beads, *Olivella* beads, numerous antler frags.	numerous bone beads, 1 hammerstone	
C-14 dates B.P.	6860 ± 170, 6660 ± 110, 5840 ± 190		3420 ± 160, 2610 ± 280, 2560 ± 80	2130 ± 80	1085 ± 60, 990 ± 140
Domestic dogs		3	1	1	1
Burials/yr.	.009	.010	.009	.008	.003
Hypoplasia rates	48%	45%	64%	66%	
Caries rates (c/p)	0.69	0.71	1.62	1.60	
Dietary content of C-3 foodstuffs	54.1% C-3	63.7% C-3	64.4% C-3	70.4% C-3	
Dietary content of CAM/C-4 foodstuffs[a]	45.9% CAM/C-4	36.3% CAM/C-4	35.6% CAM/C-4	29.6% CAM/C-4	

[a]Based on stable carbon isotope analysis.

nificant correlations and also differences are found between the two (Table 17).

The burial patterns from the San Geronimo Phase (8000–5000 B.P.) are consistent with the proposed settlement pattern of small, highly mobile groups following a generalized subsistence program. Low hypoplasia rates in the sinkhole populations from this time period are consistent with small group size (Dickel, Schulz, and McHenry 1984). The recovery of unifaces and bifaces of the types described by Weir for this phase indicate the groups were following a nonspecialized subsistence mode (Weir 1976). The recovery of the marine shell pendants is the first indication that perhaps something else is happening during this time. The marine shell could have been obtained directly from the coast by these purportedly highly mobile groups. If such a mobility pattern routinely brought these hunter-gatherers near the coast, the stable isotope analysis should have identified a marine diet component in addition to the terrestrial component. This is not the case. The isotope analysis, particularly the nitrogen isotope, does not support the possibility that the individuals contained in the level with the marine shell pendants (or any other level) had a marine component in their diet. However, it remains to be demonstrated that trade between the Edwards Plateau groups and coastal groups was established at this early time.

Additionally, the recovery of secondary burials in the San Geronimo Phase levels indicates that these societies either had certain individuals with higher status than the rest, thus deserving differential burial treatment (Binford 1971), or that the burial facility served as an aggregation site or shrine during this period (Charles and Buikstra 1983; Jirikowic 1990). Either of these two hypotheses carry cultural implications not acknowledged in Weir's constructs. The occurrence of secondary burial types and low occurrence of highly polished occlusal wear in a population dominated by pitted wear suggests that the remains of the dead were stored until such time that the seasonal round brought the group into the vicinity of the sinkhole. The dominance of the pitted wear attributed to fall/winter subsistence items suggests that the sinkhole area was scheduled for fall/winter habitation. Thus, aggregation during the fall/winter in this area probably included rites associated with the burial of the dead.

Weir proposes that the hunter-gatherer groups during the following Clear Fork Phase (5000–4000 B.P.) remained loosely structured but developed a more specialized subsistence mode and became territorially more restricted. In many respects, the data from the sinkhole suggest a continuation of the subsistence and mobility patterns established during the San Geronimo Phase. The dietary reconstruction based on dental attributes remains virtually the same. Caries rates barely increase from .69 c/p during the San Geronimo to .71 c/p during the Clear Fork. Enamel hypoplasia rates actually drop to below levels seen during the San Geronimo, suggesting reduced chronic stress. Stable isotope analysis indicates an increase in the percentage of C-3 plants in the diet from 54.5 percent during the San Geronimo to 63.7 percent. This is the only evidence to support Weir's claim that subsistence strategies changed. The wear patterns on the teeth indicate the continued use of the area during the fall/winter season. And the recovery of cremations in the burial levels during this time suggests that the burial program established for the San Geronimo Phase continued into the Clear Fork Phase. Although many aspects of the settlement and subsistence base formed a continuum with the preceding San Geronimo Phase, certain changes occurred in the social sphere. The first sign of this change was the association of unmodified deer antlers with the burial lenses. This is the first evidence that ritual artifacts were incorporated in the burial program. Prior to the Clear Fork Phase, the only evidence of ritual was the ubiquitous association of charcoal with the burial lenses. With the recovery of deer antler, the assemblage of burial goods expands from only utilitarian and personal adornment artifacts to include ritual items.

An additional association that is problematic in its interpretation is the recovery of the remains of domestic dogs with the Clear Fork Phase burials (Table 17). There is insufficient information to determine if the dogs were intentionally placed in the sinkhole as burials or in association with human burials, or if they inadvertently fell into the cavern in the same manner as their cousins the coyotes.

Hunter-gatherer groups during the subsequent Round Rock Phase (4200–2600 B.P.) are characterized by Weir as having highly structured sociopolitical structures, specialized subsistence practices targeting high-yield plant products such as acorns, and heightened territoriality. Settlement systems employed during the Round Rock are of two types: macrobands and territorially confined smaller groups (Weir 1976:130). These two systems are similar to that proposed by Charles and Buikstra (1983) for the central Mississippi area. The macrobands are equivalent to the large "sedentary" base camp groups found in the main stem of the Mississippi drainage, and the smaller groups in restricted territories are similar to the small groups found in the secondary drainages of the Mississippi system. Weir proposes that the increase in dense floral resources such as acorn-producing oak provides the staple food item necessary to support either of these two settlement systems. The artifact assemblage defines a shift toward the production of bifaces and the use of bifacial tools almost to the exclusion of unifaces.

The Bering Sinkhole Round Rock Phase burial data support many of Weir's reconstructions for this phase. To begin with, the reduction in mobility implied by either of the two settlement systems is supported by the nearly one-to-one ratio of fall/winter and spring/summer dental wear attributes. This alone suggests that the hunter-gatherer groups were within easy reach of the sinkhole burial facility throughout the year. That the size of the burial populations remained virtually the same as in the preceding phases suggests that small local groups in fixed territories occupied the area rather than large macrobands. Biological attributes that indicate shifts in settlement/subsistence modes include a 50 percent increase in the hypoplasia rate from the Clear Fork Phase and a twofold increase in the caries rates over the preceding period. The increased hypoplasia rate indicates an increase in childhood stress. Increases in stress are often attributed to reduction in mobility strategies and increases in population density (Dickel, Schulz, and McHenry 1984). The increased caries rate is consistent with the proposed increase in floral content of the diet, especially a high-carbohydrate staple such as acorns (Weir 1976) or sotol (Prewitt 1976; Wilson 1930). The increased stable carbon isotope values first seen during the Clear Fork Phase and maintained during the Round Rock Phase indicate that approximately 64.4 percent of the diet consisted of C-3 plants and animals. Both acorns and sotol are C-3 plants.

The recovery of trade items, including large, fine-grained chert biface blanks and marine shell beads, suggests that intergroup contacts were important. Another possible indicator of territoriality is the recovery of incised bone implements similar to those suggested by Hall (1988) to have served as group identifiers in southeast Texas.

The Round Rock Phase saw continued use of unmodified deer antler as a burial furnishing. The incidence of antler inclusions increases and takes on additional forms including deer skull caps with antlers still attached and burned antler.

The recovery of a cache of 14 large bifaces made by at least 3 different flintknappers is viewed as evidence for increased group investment in the burial of the dead (Bement 1991). This, plus the inclusion of bone implements with design motifs possibly signifying individual or local group identity and the increased use of deer antler, indicates that the Round Rock Phase saw the elaboration of ritual elements that began in the Clear Fork Phase. The continued presence of domestic dog only adds to the perception that reduced mobility and ritual elaboration combine with subsistence modes to suggest that the Round Rock Phase hunter-gatherers have reached a developmental plateau of complexity, termed coalescence by Weir (1976:131), not displayed by previous groups.

The subsequent San Marcos Phase (2800–1800 B.P.) marks the breakup of the system found during the Round Rock Phase. Weir characterizes the San Marcos Phase as a time of gradual decline in the pattern seen during the Round Rock Phase. He cites shifts in the diversity and intensity of lithic tool types that indicate the economy had become less specialized (Weir 1976:134). Settlement patterns become more dispersed as mobility increases. The impetus for these changes is postulated to include increased stress load due to reduced mobility and increased population density patterns. Another possibility is that contact with nomadic groups from the Plains or increased pursuit of bison that enter the Edwards Plateau area in increasing numbers during this time caused a shift in the mobility patterns and a breakdown of fixed territories (Weir 1976).

The Bering Sinkhole San Marcos Phase skeletal material provides little evidence for shifts in mobility patterns or diet during the San Marcos Phase. Enamel hypoplasia rates remain virtually unchanged at 66 percent compared to the 64 percent seen during the Round Rock Phase. Likewise, caries rates are set at 1.60 c/p compared to 1.62 c/p described for the Round Rock Phase. Tooth wear attributes remain equally divided between postulated fall/winter and spring/summer seasonal patterns. The first change is seen in the stable carbon isotope analysis. Over 70 percent of the diet was composed of C-3 plants and animals, compared with only 64.4 percent during the Round Rock Phase. Whether the increase in C-3 foodstuffs is due to a natural progression of the plant community associated with the more mesic conditions witnessed during the San Marcos Phase or changes in subsistence practices cannot be determined with the information at hand.

Telling changes are seen in the artifacts. The San Marcos Phase deposits did not contain any of the incised bone implements or any trade items such as the marine shell beads and large bifaces recovered from the Round Rock Phase deposits. Likewise, no unmodified deer antler was recovered. The dearth of these materials in the San Marcos Phase levels suggests that mortuary and possibly social changes had occurred.

The final phase of the Archaic is the Twin Sisters (2000–700 B.P.). Weir postulates that during this period, hunter-gatherer groups were loosely structured. Settlement patterns were similar to those proposed for the San Geronimo Phase, consisting of small, widely scattered sites occupied by small, highly mobile groups.

This phase marks the last use of Bering Sinkhole as a mortuary site. Unfortunately, the reconstruction of the population and cultural characteristics for this period has been hampered by the recovery of few provenienced materials from the sinkhole. What is apparent, however, is that fewer burials were deposited in the sinkhole, and these burials were impoverished in the amount of associated burial goods.

Neither of the two individuals available for study had hypoplasias. The caries rate drops from the 1.60 c/p defined in the San Marcos Phase to 1.00 c/p during the Twin Sisters. The interpretive value of this data is hampered by the extremely small sample size ($n = 2$), but the reduction in caries rate suggests that the diet became less dependent on high-carbohydrate foodstuffs and probably became more mixed.

The mortuary evidence from Bering Sinkhole generally supports the cultural constructs proposed by Weir (1976) based on data obtained from site and artifact attributes. The sinkhole provides evidence for change in the social as well as subsistence/settlement sphere, particularly during the Round Rock Phase.

Evidence for Ritual Elaboration

Perhaps the most important contribution made by the investigation of the Bering Sinkhole mortuary deposits is the ability to track the elaboration of ritual against the backdrop of subsistence and settlement patterns. One recurrent theme identified by cross-cultural studies of mortuary practices is the tie between death and fertility and how these two concepts are ritually manifest (Bloch and Parry 1982).

> . . . in most cases what would seem to be revitalised in funerary practices is that resource which is *culturally conceived* to be most essential to the reproduction of the social order. (Bloch and Parry 1982:8)

Thus, it is not human fertility that is emphasized but rather key aspects of the natural or social environment.

In Woodburn's (1982) ethnographic study of four African hunter-gatherer societies, he demonstrated that it was not the reproduction of the people that was emphasized, but rather the ability to appropriate nature. Ethnographic studies have the advantage of being able to view all aspects of the mortuary program. Whether archaeologists can determine which resources were emphasized in burial rituals depends on their ability to reconstruct the ritual aspects of the burial program.

At Bering Sinkhole, ritual activity is most evident in the post-4000 B.P. Clear Fork and Round Rock levels. Here it is manifest in unmodified and often burned deer antlers, incised bone implements, chert trade blanks, and marine shell trade beads.

Antlers are used in rituals throughout the world and are logical items for ritual significance in hunter-gatherer groups that rely on deer as a major source of protein. Although antler is important for tool production, it is also readily available throughout much of the year either on animals or shed across the landscape. Thus, the use of large quantities of antler as a burial furnishing removes neither a prized nor limited resource from circulation. The significance of the antler stems from its ritual context, probably derived from the importance of deer as a food source, especially during times of aggregation and feasts.

That deer hunting was a prestige activity is likely. Anyone proficient in deer hunting may have also achieved a certain status. If deer provided the major protein source, then the passing of a successful deer hunter could put a strain on the social order until a proficient hunter replaced him. A ritual such as that performed by certain groups in northern Mexico (Griffen 1969:131), where trophy deer heads kept by the deceased hunter were burned to distribute hunting skill and prowess to the rest of the group, would act as a regeneration of a necessary resource, that is, hunting skill (Bloch and Parry 1982:7). Ellen (1988:132), in studying the Nuaulu of central Seram, suggests that inedible portions of valued food were used to represent ownership of that resource within an area and as a symbol of the social relations of consumption of the edible parts. Thus, the deer antler may have functioned as a symbol of the social contracts between the hunter and other members of the society or with neighboring groups. At present, it cannot be demonstrated that the antler found in the sinkhole deposits and at other burial localities in Texas served such a function. However, such a purpose would be consistent with the reconstruction suggested by other aspects of the sinkhole burial population. The incised bone implements may indicate that group membership reification was another regenerative theme in the burial program (Hall 1988).

The cache of 1 drill and 14 bifaces, apparently made by at least 3 different flintknappers, seems to indicate that the fine-grained chert resources were important. The conclusion that large biface blanks were used in trade with areas off the Edwards Plateau provides social as well as economic importance to this resource by supplying intergroup contacts. The recovery of marine shell beads in the same deposits containing the biface cache demonstrates the social sanctification of exchange with groups to the south and east.

Sinkhole Sites as the Edwards Plateau Equivalent of Southeast Texas Mortuary Sites

Sinkhole burial sites have the potential to supply information about the mortuary and biological aspects of hunter-gatherer groups in Texas that, until now, has only been obtainable from the more conventional mortuary sites from southeast Texas. In particular, the skeletal materials are usually well preserved, having been deposited in deep underground caverns that have constant temperature, humidity, and soil conditions. The often heightened preservation of the bone itself allows for the identification of subtle pathological indicators that tell of the health, nutrition, and lifeways of the living population. Dental patterns of wear and disease also provide information on the eating habits and general health of the individual.

The stratified deposits in the sinkhole provide insights into the ritualistic behavior associated with the burial of the dead. The use of Bering Sinkhole—an isolated geologic feature at least .75 kilometer from the nearest habitation site—in itself indicates a social sanctification of the site as a burial ground. In this respect, this sinkhole joins other sites in fulfilling a technical aspect of cemeteries: that is, the use of a defined area separate from areas of everyday activities (Binford 1971; Goldstein 1980:8). In the conventional mortuary sites east of the plateau, deer antler, incised bone implements, chert materials including large thin bifaces and cores, exotic materials, and, to a lesser extent, dog bones have been recovered. Bering Sinkhole has produced all of these materials.

The funerary assemblage at Bering contained many of the same types of artifacts, although not in as large a quantity as that found at Loma Sandia and Ernest Witte. At Loma Sandia alone, an estimated 142 caches were recovered with over 110 burials. Bone beads, shell ornaments, unmodified antlers, and large bifaces were among this site's burial furnishings. The commonality of the Bering Sinkhole grave goods with those of more traditional mortuary sites strengthens the characterization of the sinkhole as a sanctified burial ground rather than a corpse repository.

In addition, the stratified deposits of the sinkhole present a diachronic framework from which to view the development and elaboration of the ritual use of these materials. The use of fire (not associated with cremations) in conjunction with the interment of the dead is found in all burial levels. Likewise, cores and bifaces of the high-quality local cherts are found throughout the deposits. However, in the older deposits only one or two items are found in each burial zone, while in the 3,100-year-old level, chert cobbles, cores, and the cache of large bifaces were found. Concentrations of deer antlers were recovered from 4,000-year-old deposits. Their frequency increased in the 3,400-to-2,700-year-old levels. During this same span, burned antlers and incised bone implements appear.

As already mentioned, the postdepositional disarticulation and distribution of skeletal materials in the sinkhole preclude the direct association of materials with specific individuals. However, the more conventional burial sites of Archaic age to the east illustrate the extent reached in the elaboration of the ritual theme involving fine-grained chert, deer antler, and the use of fire. At the Olmos Dam site, estimated at 2,000 years old, the flexed bodies of adults were often completely covered with unmodified deer antlers (Lukowski 1988). At this same site, two infant burials were separated by a hearthlike feature: one infant was covered by chert cores and cobbles, and the other, by antlers—including burned antlers. Apparently, a ritual utilizing fire and antlers, in conjunction with highly valued chert materials, was conducted at the time of burial of these two infants.

The recovery of boatstones made of material from the Ouachita Mountains of Arkansas, graphite and biotite schist from the central Texas mineral region, fine-grained chert from the Edwards Plateau, and large conch shell pendants possibly from the Florida coast prompted Hall (1981:302) to propose that the Late Archaic hunter-gatherer groups on the Gulf Coastal Plain of Texas participated in an import-export relationship with southeastern cultures. Hall hypothesizes that:

> During the Middle Archaic, basically isolated groups subsisted through hunting and gathering pursuits adapted to the particular localized environments wherein they operated. Though there were striking similarities between the limited array of artifacts from region to region, most objects seem to have been manufactured from locally available resources.

> Expanding Late Archaic and Woodland populations in Texas and throughout the eastern United States (brought on by efficient use and abundant supplies of plant and animal foods) resulted in greatly improved systems of communication and transport. A wide variety of artifacts and raw materials were circulated across half the continent, connecting such divergent points as the Florida

Gulf Coast and the Ouachita Mountains with the western reaches of the import-export sphere in central Texas. The Late Archaic and Woodland groups across the eastern half of Texas both received from, and contributed to, the system.

Sometime in the period between 50 B.C. and A.D. 200 along the western periphery of the import-export sphere in Texas, pressures were exerted on local populations which triggered the gradual but inexorable retraction of the sphere northeastward across central Texas and the coastal plain to eventually reach the much reduced area of east Texas where participation continued on into Late Prehistoric (Caddoan) times. (Hall 1981:302–303)

Accompanying participation in the import-export sphere, was a shift in the size and complexity of mortuary sites. The Middle Archaic burial group at Ernest Witte contained an estimated 61 individuals compared to over 145 individuals in the Late Archaic burial group (Hall 1981:281). Terminal Archaic and Late Prehistoric burial groups at Ernest Witte contained 9 and 13 individuals, respectively (Hall 1981:274). Whether the increase in burial population size represents an increase in actual living population numbers or a shift in settlement/mobility patterns has not been determined. Hall (1981, n.d.) proposes that increased reliance on high-yield, storable foodstuffs such as pecans made large-scale aggregation of hunter-gatherer groups possible. The reduced number of burials in the terminal Archaic and Late Prehistoric components at Ernest Witte suggest that another shift in population or settlement patterns occurred.

At Bering Sinkhole, burial numbers did not increase during the Late Archaic as they did at Ernest Witte, and ritual elaboration occurred during the Middle Archaic rather than during the Late Archaic. In fact, the burial program at Bering Sinkhole suggests a decline in ritual activity during the Late Archaic. Exotic materials were recovered from Bering Sinkhole, but these materials were limited to marine shell that probably came from the Texas Gulf Coast. The marine shell artifacts predate similar specimens from Ernest Witte by at least 500 years for the beads and 5,000 years for the pendants.

Rituals, employing deer antler, fine-grained chert, incised bone implements, and fire, developed during the Round Rock Phase on the Edwards Plateau apparently continued in use during the Late Archaic in coastal plain sites (Lukowski 1988; Hall 1981; Taylor and Highley n.d.). Whether the ritual similarities are a product of independent development or diffusion from the plateau groups to the coastal plain groups cannot be determined at the present time.

The investigation of Bering Sinkhole has provided the opportunity to track dietary, health, and ritual changes in prehistoric groups on the Edwards Plateau of central Texas through time. Through the consideration of models of hunter-gatherer subsistence and mobility, changes in cultural structure or organization have been identified. Perhaps the most important result of this study has been the ability to integrate the burial practices with the material culture, subsistence modes, and mobility patterns to create a more complete history of the prehistoric inhabitants of central Texas.

In conclusion, the careful excavation and study of the Bering Sinkhole mortuary site has shown that serious consideration of sinkhole burial sites as a component of a regional mortuary practice produces comparable information to that gained from the more traditional burial sites in southeast Texas, although at a reduced scale. The further consideration of sinkhole burial sites will provide interesting and viable insights into the lifeways of prehistoric groups. The investigation at Bering Sinkhole raises some very intriguing questions that cannot be adequately addressed at our current level of knowledge about North American prehistoric cultures. Bering Sinkhole is an example of the use of subsurface features through time by various hunter-gatherer cultures. That this sinkhole and many others are not part of any habitation site suggests that such features are part of a sacred landscape that pervades the belief systems of at least the hunter-gatherer groups of central Texas, southwest Texas, and northern Mexico. Does the use of vertical shaft sinkholes from California to Alabama reflect a pan-American belief in the sanctity of subsurface vaults, or do sinkholes simply present a practical, labor-efficient method of disposing of the dead? By incorporating burial programs with subsistence, mobility, and organizational studies, we begin to better understand the pervasiveness of certain belief systems in many prehistoric societies.

Appendix. Accounting of Species

Class Reptilia

Chrysemys concina   Turtle Carapace
Material: Carapace
Distribution: Level 38

The pattern on the neural and costal bone plates and the low dome of this carapace most closely resembles the Texas slider (*Chrysemys concina texana*) in the comparative collection at the TMM-VP. The Texas slider belongs to the family Emydidae that consists of freshwater and semiterrestrial turtles composed of an estimated 30 genera and 85 species. Unlike the land tortoises, Emydidae turtles have hind feet adapted for swimming (Stebbins 1966). Turtles of this family inhabit primarily freshwater, although a few species are found in brackish water. Another characteristic of many emydid turtles is that they bask in the sun on logs and rocks that protrude from the water. The Texas slider ranges in size from 18 to 25 centimeters in length with the largest at 27.3 centimeters. This species lives primarily in rivers, although specimens have been collected from ditches and cattle tanks of central Texas, along the Pecos River to southeastern New Mexico and south into Coahuila, Nuevo Leon, and Tamaulipas, Mexico, and extreme south Texas (Stebbins 1966).

Class Mammalia

Didelphis virginiana (Kerr)   Opossum
Material: 1 mandible (LI–M4), 1 maxilla (RP4, M1, M2)
Distribution: Level 1

Opossums occupy a wide range of habitats including woodlands, prairies, and marshes. Their present statewide range includes all but the far west areas bordering New Mexico. The lack of woody vegetation seems to be the only limiting factor in their distribution (Davis 1978).

Dasypus novemcinctus (Linnaeus)   Nine-banded armadillo
Material: Numerous scutes
Distribution: Level 1

Dasypus novemcinctus is easily identifiable in Texas by its distinctive scutes that compose its armored shell. The armadillo lives in varied habitats that contain soils that support the insects and animals it feeds upon. Thus, it is found throughout the eastern half of the state (Davis 1978:269). Armadillos are a recent addition to the fauna of Texas, first entering the state about 1850 and gradually moving northward onto the Edwards Plateau by 1905 (Buchanan and Talmadge 1954).

Lepus californicus Gray   Black-tailed jackrabbit
Material: 34 mandibles, 25 maxillae
Distribution: Levels 1, 18, 20, 23, 24, 25, 26, 27, 28, 29, 30, 31, 32, 33, 34, 35, 37, 40, 41

The jackrabbit was identified through the application of discriminant function equations developed by Hulbert (1984) to distinguish between various *Lepus* and *Sylvilagus* species. With the exception of the East Texas Piney Woods, the black-tailed jackrabbit is found throughout Texas (Davis 1978:237). It lives in greatest numbers in the dry, desert regions of western Texas. The wide range of habitats occupied by the jackrabbit limits the usefulness of this species in environmental reconstruction.

Sylvilagus sp.   Cottontail rabbit
Material: 296 mandibles, 169 maxillae
Distribution: Levels 1, 2, 3, 15, 16, 17, 18, 19, 20, 22, 23, 24, 25, 26, 27, 28, 29, 30, 31, 32, 33, 34, 35, 36, 37, 38, 39, 40, 41

Four species of *Sylvilagus* occur in Texas today (Davis 1978:239–242). Discriminant functions, developed by Hulbert (1984), can be applied to the dentitions to segregate the four species and to segregate them from *Lepus* sp. *S. robustus* is found in the mountainous areas of the Trans-Pecos, and *S. aquaticus* is found east of the Balcones Fault zone. The remaining two species, *S. floridanus* (Allen) and *S. audubonii* (Baird), have overlapping modern ranges that include the Edwards Plateau region. *S. audubonii* is usually found in grassy, often arid habitats, while *S. floridanus* is adapted to wetter habitats with dense brushy cover. Kerr County is at the eastern boundary of the modern *S. audubonii* range.

Spermophilus mexicanus (Erxleben)   Mexican ground squirrel
Material: 1 skull, 7 mandibles, 5 maxillae
Distribution: Levels 22, 25, 29, 30, 32, 34, 35, 38, 41, 42

Species identification depended on the morphological comparisons between the Bering sample and various *Spermophilus* and *Citellus* materials at the Vertebrate Paleontology Laboratory, TMM, the University of Texas at Austin. The Bering specimens consistently fell within the size range of the *Spermophilus mexicanus* comparative samples. Mexican ground squirrels are found in brushy and grassy terrain with primarily sandy or gravelly soils (Davis 1978:149). Its current range in Texas is the Edwards Plateau, Trans-Pecos, and south Texas physiographic zones. This ground squirrel often utilizes the burrows of gophers whose range it overlaps. It is a favorite food of the badger.

Thomomys bottae (Exdoux and Gervais)   Botta's pocket gopher
Material: 11 mandibles
Distribution: Levels 20, 23, 25, 29, 34, 39, 40, 41, 42

This gopher can be identified by the presence of an enamel plate on the posterior surface of the upper premolar, enamel plates on both anterior and posterior faces of the lower molars, and the teardrop shape of the molars. Botta's pocket gopher is a medium-sized rodent that has fur-lined, exterior cheek pouches from which it draws its name. This gopher inhabits widely varied soil types ranging from loose sands to dense clays in deserts, grasslands, and mountain environments (Schmidly 1977:20; Davis 1978:164). It is found primarily in the western Edwards Plateau and Trans-Pecos regions of Texas. Dalquest, Roth, and Judd (1969) report no recent occurrences of this genus in the area today, but it is well represented in deposits of Holocene age.

Geomys bursarius (Shaw)   Plains pocket gopher
Material: 1 skull (LP4–M3, RM1), 1 mandible (LI–M3), 1 maxilla (E)
Distribution: Levels 30, 32

Unlike *Thomomys*, the upper premolars of *Geomys* lack enamel on their posterior surfaces, and the lower molars have enamel plates only on their posterior surfaces. The upper premolars of *Geomys* can be separated from *Pappogeomys* due to their inferior size. These pocket gophers inhabit sandy soils where the topsoil is more than 10 centimeters deep. Current distribution of this gopher in Texas includes the eastern Edwards Plateau where soil depth is sufficient for burrowing (Davis 1978:166).

Pappogeomys castanops (Baird)   Yellow-faced pocket gopher
Material: 1 mandible (I, M1, M3), 1 maxilla (RP4, LP4–M2)
Distribution: Levels 26, 29

Pappogeomys have enamel plates on the posterior surface of the upper premolars, as do *Geomys*; however, the greater size of *Pappogeomys* easily tells the two apart. These large pocket gophers inhabit deep soils free from rocks. Their current distribution in Texas includes the western third of the state from the Panhandle to Maverick County along the Rio Grande. Kerr County is currently east of their range, although adjacent Edwards County is within the range (Davis 1978: 171).

Perognathus sp.   Pocket mouse
Material: 17 mandibles
Distribution: Levels 19, 20, 22, 25, 26, 28, 29, 31, 33, 34, 36, 38, 39

Eight species of *Perognathus* have been reported in Texas (Davis 1978:172–182). Only two, *P. merriami* and *Chaetodipus hispidus*, currently range on the Edwards Plateau including Kerr County. *P. merriami* is smaller than *C. hispidus*, and the Bering Sinkhole material best fits the larger species. Both species are found in areas of sandy, friable soils.

Microtus sp.   Voles
Material: 1 mandible (LI–M3), 2 maxillae (R&LM1, M2; R&LM2)
Distribution: Levels 6, 18, 19

The three specimens exhibit characteristics midway between *M. ochrogaster* and *M. pinetorum*. Specifically, the mandibular M1 is shaped more similar to *M. ochrogaster*. One skull fragment and maxilla has a least width in the *pinetorum* range, but the nasal length is within the *ochrogaster* range. The third specimen, a maxilla, contains no diagnostic characters. Given the extremely small sample size and the inconclusive nature of what few characteristics can be measured, it appears that species determination is not warranted. Historically, the area including Kerr and Edwards counties has supported a colony of *M. pinetorum* (Davis 1978), and evidence from Schulze Cave and Halls Cave indicates that *M. ochrogaster* withdrew from this area early in the Holocene prior to 5,000 years ago (Dalquest, Roth, and Judd 1969; Toomey 1990). Since the Bering microtines are from post-1,000-year-old deposits, it is most likely that they belong to *M. pinetorum*.

The pine vole is found in woodland areas with sufficient ground clutter and grasses to conceal their shallow burrows and trails. These mice subsist primarily on roots and tubers supplemented by acorns and other nuts (Davis 1978:224). Pine voles have recently inhabited an area of the Edwards Plateau that includes Gillespie, Edwards, and Kerr counties, although their main range is in northeast Texas (Bryant 1941; Davis 1978).

Peromyscus sp.   Mouse
Material: 35 mandibles, 2 maxillae
Distribution: Levels 18, 19, 22, 24, 29, 30, 31, 32, 34, 35, 36, 37, 38, 41

Nine species of *Peromyscus* have been identified in Texas (Davis 1978: 199–211). Four of these currently range into portions of the Edwards Plateau that include Kerr County (*P. maniculatus, P. leucopus, P. attwateri,* and *P. pectoralis*). The Bering Sinkhole materials could not be identified at the species level. Two, *P. maniculatus* and *P. leucopus,* inhabit forested areas including riparian zones, while *P. attwateri* and *P. pectoralis* are found primarily in rocky terrain.

Onychomys leucogaster (Wied)   Northern or short-tailed
                                  grasshopper mouse
Material: 6 mandibles (LI; LI; LI, M1; LI–M3; RI; RI, M1)
Distribution: Levels 16, 19, 31, 32, 35, 37

Onychomys is easily identified by the pronounced posteriorly turned coronoid process and the high-cusped mandibular molars (Dalquest, Roth, and Judd 1969). The northern grasshopper mouse is a stout-bodied, short-tailed mouse that inhabits grasslands or open brush-lands with sandy or powdery soils (Davis 1978:193). Its current distribution in Texas is predominantly in the Southern Plains, Trans-Pecos, and southern Texas physiographic regions. Its presence in a faunal assemblage may indicate a desert or grassland environmental setting (Schmidly 1977:21).

Neotoma sp.   Woodrat
Material: 153 mandibles, 54 maxillae
Distribution: Levels 11, 20, 23, 24, 25, 26, 27, 28, 29, 30, 31, 32, 33, 34, 35, 36, 37, 38, 39, 40

Various techniques have been proposed to distinguish between the different species at the skeletal level. One widely used method to seg-regate *N. albigula* and *N. micropus* is the width of the second loph of the /M1 (Dalquest, Roth, and Judd 1969). However recently, this method has proved to be unreliable on many Texas specimens (Rosenberg 1985; Winans 1989). In an attempt to refine the technique, a crown height measurement of the /M1 was added to identify any vagaries in the width measurement that might be attributable to differential tooth wear patterns or age of the individual. Simple regression analysis identified a tendency for a negative correlation of width and crown height but the variables could account for only 4 percent of the observed variance.

The identification of *N. mexicanus* specimens based on the presence of a dentine track on the /M1 was also attempted, but this attribute was not found in the Bering sample. Thus, no *N. mexicanus* individuals were identified. Four species of *Neotoma* are known to occur in Texas. Two, *N. albigula* and *N. micropus*, inhabit brushlands in desert or near-desert areas. *N. mexicana* is found in rocky areas of the Trans-Pecos, and *N. floridana* inhabits a wide range of niches including swamplands, arid plains, and forests.

Sigmodon hispidus Say and Ord   Hispid cotton rat
Material: 10 mandibles (I–M3), 1 maxilla (M1, M2)
Distribution: Levels 1, 6, 15, 17, 19, 20, 23, 28, 32, 34, 41

The cotton rat was easily identified based on the S-design of the dentine on the /M3. The lack of other *Sigmodon* species on the Edwards Plateau suggests that the Bering specimens belong to *Sigmodon hispidus*. This robust, moderately large rat inhabits tall grasslands and prairies and has been reported in all parts of Texas (Davis 1978: 213–215). This species is an indicator of grassland or riparian habitats with deep sandy soils (Schmidly 1977: 15, 21).

Notiosorex crawfordi (Coues)   Desert shrew
Material: 3 mandibles (LI–M3; LI–M3; RI–M3)
Distribution: Levels 27, 35, 38

The desert shrew is distinguished from other shrews on the presence of only three unicuspid teeth on each side of the maxilla, deep-notched articular condyle on the mandible, and by the relative dearth of red pigment on the tooth crowns (Dalquest, Roth, and Judd 1969). The desert shrew is found in habitats varying from xeric areas to wetlands (Davis 1978: 42). Its current range includes Kerr County and areas to the north, south, and west.

Mustela frenata (Lichtenstein)   Long-tailed weasel
Material: 1 mandible of a juvenile
Distribution: Level 25

The mandible and erupting permanent teeth were compared with *Mustela frenata* and *Mustela erminea* jaws in the collection housed at the TMM. The morphology of the erupting crowns and size of the mandible were more similar to *Mustela frenata*. Long-tailed weasels are found in a variety of habitats including the East Texas Piney Woods, southern Edwards Plateau, southern Texas, and Trans-Pecos physiographic zones (Davis 1978:98). Their range overlaps those of pocket gophers and ground squirrels on which they feed and whose burrows they usurp for dens.

Conepatus mesoleucus (Lichtenstein)   Hog-nosed skunk
Material: 1 mandible (LP2–M1) and /M1
Distribution: Level 29

The identification of these specimens rests on the large size of the teeth when compared to *Mephitis* and the greater depth of the mandible. The hog-nosed skunk is a large skunk that inhabits sparsely timbered, rocky terrain. In Texas they have been reported from the mountainous area of the Trans-Pecos, across the limestone region of the Edwards Plateau, and into the Big Thicket country of east Texas (Davis 1978:112–113). As is evident by their wide distribution across Texas, the hog-nosed skunk cannot be used as a primary environmental indicator. However, this skunk is not common in densely wooded areas or in riparian habitats (Schmidly 1977:21).

Taxidea taxus (Schreber)   Badger
Material: Complete skull and jaw, /P4, /P3, I3/, P3/, C/
Distribution: Levels 25, 28, 30, 35

Taxidea taxus is easily identified on the basis of the triangular shaped M1/ and the high metaconid on the /P4. Overall, the dentitions are quite robust and morphologically distinctive from other carnivores. The badger is found in a variety of habitats ranging from the southern coast, south Texas, Edwards Plateau, Trans-Pecos, and Southern Plains physiographic zones. They are most common, however, in the dry prairies of west Texas (Davis 1978:114), where they rely on ground squirrels and prairie dogs as a dominant food source. Additional food sources include cottontails, pocket gophers, and other burrowing rodents.

Canis familiaris   Domestic dog
Material: 2 mandibles, 1 maxilla, 3 M1/, 4 P4/, 2 /M2, /M1, /P2, 2 /C, /I3
Distribution: Levels 20, 23, 26, 28, 29, 30

The *C. familiaris* dentitions are smaller in dimensions than those of *C. latrans*. This trend holds true for tooth size, mandible, and maxillary length and depth. Although *C. familiaris* usually is characterized by well-spaced tooth rows and greater mandibular depth, compared with *C. latrans*, the crowded tooth rows and shallow mandibular depth characterize the smaller *C. familiaris* varieties (Olsen 1974). The Bering Sinkhole *C. familiaris* are small-jawed, short-snouted animals. Nonmetric attributes that differentiate the *C. familiaris* from *C. latrans* include the crowding of mandibular cheek teeth, crowding of the mandibular incisors, and the congenital absence of the lower P1. Another difference is the "back turned" apex of the coronoid process of the ascending ramus in dogs (Olsen 1974:534). In combination, these attributes describe a dog that is smaller in overall size than a coyote, has crowded upper and lower tooth rows, and has reduced snout length. One individual in particular is brachycephalic to an extent comparable to a modern bulldog (Sisson and Grossman 1950).

Canis latrans Say   Coyote
Material: horizontal ramus /M2, 4 /I3, 2 /P2, 3 /P3, 5 /P4, /M1, /C, 5 I3/, 5 P3/, 3 P4/, 6 M1/, 2 M2/, 2 C/
Distribution: Levels 21, 23, 25, 26, 27, 28, 29, 30, 31, 32, 33, 34, 37, 38, 39, 40

The coyote has been identified based on comparing the size ranges of the tooth rows and individual teeth with published sizes of modern coyotes (Nowak 1979). The coyote occupies varied habitats including desert scrub, grasslands, and forests, and, except in areas of intense trapping, it is currently found throughout Texas (Davis 1978:124). The natural food of a coyote consists predominantly of rabbits, rodents, reptiles, and carrion. Although dens are usually dug into hillsides, they can consist of enlarged badger burrows, rocky crevices, or caves.

Canis lupus (Linnaeus)   Gray wolf
Material: 1 skull, 4 mandibles, /C, 2/P2, /p3
Distribution: Levels 1, 2, 3, 4, 7, 16, 25, 30

The gray wolf has been identified based on the measurements of tooth size compared to modern gray wolf and red wolf ranges (Nowak 1979). Gray wolves were once widespread in Texas, following closely the large herds of buffalo, and have been extirpated from most areas of the state in response to predation on domestic livestock.

Procyon lotor (Linnaeus)   Raccoon
Material: 2 mandibles including I through M2; mandible with DI3, DP1, DP3, DM1; 1 edentulous maxilla fragment; /C; /P3; /P4; 2 /M1; 4 /M2; I2/; 2 C/; 3 M1/; M2/
Distribution: Levels 23, 24, 25, 26, 28, 31, 32, 33, 35, 36, 38, 39

The low-cusped cheek teeth distinguish this carnivore from other comparable-sized taxa. The Bering Sinkhole specimens are at the upper range of or larger than modern raccoons on the Edwards Plateau (Table 18). Many dental characteristics, including wear facets on the /C, and generally more robust dentition are similar to attributes known for *P. lotor simus* (Wright and Lundelius 1963; Arata and Hutchison 1964). Larger raccoons consistently predate modern-sized raccoons across Texas and appear to have been replaced by the latter by 1,000 years ago (Wright and Lundelius 1963). Wright and Lundelius attribute the succession to the smaller raccoon as a continuation of the trend since the Pleistocene toward smaller varieties within a taxa. Large *Procyon* species or subspecies occur today in more northern latitudes including Oregon and Idaho. The sinkhole produced large-sized individuals from 7,600 years ago to approximately 2,500 years ago. The absence of post-2,500-year-old specimens precludes the assessment of the size reduction pattern proposed by Wright and Lundelius (1963).

Raccoons inhabit all regions of Texas, and their only limiting factor is the availability of surface water (Davis 1978:91). They are most numerous in broadleaf woodlands and usually den in hollow trees. Raccoons consume insects, invertebrates, fish, birds, snakes, nuts, and fruits.

Ursus americanus Pallas   Black bear
Material: mandible (RM1–M3), claw
Distribution: Levels 23, 38

The black bear was identified based on the smaller size of the teeth when compared to the modern tooth-size ranges of brown or grizzly bears. Black bears inhabit forest areas, woodlands, and dense thickets along waterways. Their current distribution in Texas is limited to the mountainous region of the Trans-Pecos. However, within the last century, black bears were found throughout much of the state (Davis 1978:90). Although omnivorous, black bears rely heavily on a diet of

Table 18. Comparison of the Measurements of Prehistoric Raccoon Mandibular Dentitions from Bering Sinkhole with Modern Samples from Texas and Oregon

Level	C Length (mm)	C Width (mm)	P4 Ramus Depth	M1 Ramus Depth	M2 Ramus Depth	M1 Length (mm)	M1 Anter. Width	M1 Post. Width	M2 Length (mm)	M2 Anter. Width	M2 Post. Width
24	9.0	5.4	14.8	13.8	14.2	11.3	5.9	6.9	12.2	6.0	6.0
25	6.8	4.7							12.3	6.3	6.2
26						10.3	5.5	6.3			
34									9.8	5.4	5.5
36									11.2	6.5	6.5
39	8.3	5.4	15.3	15.6	16.0	10.9	6.5	7.3	11.6	6.7	6.4
39						12.7	6.7	6.4			
39	8.3	6.1									
40	7.3	5.5							11.7	6.0	6.2
Texas[a]	6.3 ± .12	4.3 ± .09	12.0 ± .21	11.9 ± .19	13.0 ± .22	10.0 ± .07	6.2 ± .10	6.6 ± .08	9.7 ± .12	5.8 ± .07	5.7 ± .07
Oregon[a]	7.5 ± .32	5.7 ± .24	14.2 ± .08	14.1 ± .08	15.6 ± .07	10.3 ± .18	6.4 ± .11	7.0 ± .20	10.2 ± .16	6.3 ± .09	5.8 ± .05

[a]Recent sample ranges are from Wright and Lundelius (1963).

insects and plants. They have been known to kill and eat young deer and comparable-sized livestock and occasionally snack on carrion.

Odocoileus cf. *O. virginianus* Boddaert   White-tailed deer
Material: 2 mandibles, /M3, 2 /M2, /M1, M2/, M1/, M3/; 33 antler fragments; 3 burned antler fragments; 1 skull fragment with attached antler bases
Distribution: Levels 12, 13, 14, 23, 24, 25, 26, 27, 28, 29, 36, 38

The deer material from Bering Sinkhole is tentatively identified as white-tailed based on the recovery of only unforked antler segments. However, due to the fragmented condition of the antlers, it is possible that forked segments were not preserved. The deer remains from nearby Schulze Cave were all identified as white-tailed deer, although no justification is given (Dalquest, Roth, and Judd 1969).

Bison bison   Bison
Material: P2/, 2 hooves
Distribution: Levels 5, 10, 11

The bovid material is identified as *Bison* on the basis of the vertical distribution of materials. The tooth and hooves are larger than deer or elk and fall within the range of either *Bison bison* or *Bos* sp. The deposits are less than 1,000 years old, thus precluding the possible occurrence of *Bison antiquus* or other forms that became extinct during early Holocene times. This material is not modern and thus not attributed to *Bos* on the basis of estimated sedimentation rates proposed for the upper Unit I deposits (see chapter 3, "Dating the Deposits"). A rate of .15 cm/yr provides an estimated age range of from 350 to 750 B.P., prior to the introduction of cattle into the Edwards Plateau region. Bison remains have been found at numerous sites on the plateau during this time frame (Dillehay 1974).

References Cited

Abbott, P. L., and C. M. Woodruff, Jr.
1986 The Balcones Escarpment: Geology, Hydrology, Ecology, and Social Development in Central Texas. Paper presented at the annual meeting of the Geological Society of America, San Antonio.

Andrews, Jean
1981 *Texas Shells: A Field Guide.* Austin: University of Texas Press.

Antevs, Ernst
1955 Geologic-Climatic Dating in the West. *American Antiquity* 20(4):317–335.

Arata, A. A., and J. H. Hutchison
1964 The Raccoon (Procyon) in the Pleistocene of North America. *Tulane Studies in Geology* 2(2):21–27.

Aveleyra, L., M. Maldonado, and P. Martinez
1956 *Cueva de la Candelaria.* Mexico City: Memorias del Instituto Nacional de Antropología e Historia V.

Barnes, Virgil E.
1981 *Geologic Atlas of Texas, Llano Sheet.* Bureau of Economic Geology, University of Texas at Austin.

Bartel, Brad
1982 A Historical Review of Ethnological and Archaeological Analyses of Mortuary Practice. *Journal of Anthropological Archaeology* 1(1):32–58.

Bass, William M.
1987 *Human Osteology: A Laboratory and Field Manual.* Special Publication No. 2. Columbia: Missouri Archaeological Society.

Bement, Leland C.
1985a Spray Foam: A New Bone Encasement Technique. *Journal of Field Archaeology* 12(3):371–372.
1985b Archeological Investigations in Seminole Sink. In *Seminole Sink: Excavation of a Vertical Shaft Tomb, Val Verde County, Texas.* Compiled by Solveig A. Turpin. Research Report 93. Austin: Texas Archeological Survey, University of Texas.
1987 Ephemeral Site Morphology: Fuller Shelter (41KY27), Kinney County, Texas. *La Tierra* 14(4):5–23.

1991 The Thunder Valley Burial Cache: Group Investment in a Central Texas Sinkhole Cemetery. *Plains Anthropologist* 36(135):97–109.

Benfer, R., and A. Benfer

1962 A Vertical Cave Burial in Uvalde County, Texas. *Texas Caver* 7:41–42.

1981 The Mason Ranch Burial Cave, Uvalde County, Texas. *La Tierra* 8(3): 16–26.

Bering, August C., IV

1987 Personal communication relating the condition of the sinkhole upon discovery.

Berryman, Hugh E., Douglas W. Owsley, and Avery M. Henderson

1979 Non-Carious Interproximal Grooves in Arikara Indian Dentitions. *American Journal of Physical Anthropology* 50:209–212.

Binford, Lewis R.

1971 Mortuary Practices: Their Study and Their Potential. In *Approaches to the Social Dimensions of Mortuary Practices*. Edited by James A. Brown. *Memoir of the Society for American Archaeology* 25:6–29.

1980 Willow Smoke and Dogs' Tails: Hunter-Gatherer Settlement Systems and Archeological Site Formation. *American Antiquity* 45:4–20.

Birdsell, Joseph B.

1968 Some Predictions for the Pleistocene System among Recent Hunters and Gatherers. In *Man the Hunter*. Edited by Richard Lee and Irven DeVore. Chicago: Aldine Publishing Company.

Black, Stephen L., and A. J. McGraw

1985 *The Panther Springs Creek Site: Cultural Change and Continuity within the Upper Salado Creek Watershed, South-Central Texas.* Archaeological Survey Report 100. San Antonio: Center for Archaeological Research, University of Texas at San Antonio.

Blair, Frank W.

1950 The Biotic Provinces of Texas. *Texas Journal of Science* 2(1):93–117.

Bloch, Maurice, and Jonathan Parry

1982 *Death and the Regeneration of Life.* Cambridge: Cambridge University Press.

Boutton, T. W., P. D. Klein, M. J. Lynott, J. E. Price, and L. L. Tieszen

1984 Stable Carbon Isotope Ratios as Indicators of Prehistoric Human Diet. In *Stable Isotopes in Nutrition*. Edited by J. R. Turnlund and P. E. Johnson. Pp. 191–204. Washington, D.C.: ACS Symposium Series.

Brothwell, D. R.

1981 *Digging Up Bones.* Ithaca: Cornell University Press.

Brown, Tasman, and Stephen Molnar

1990 Interproximal Grooving and Task Activity in Australia. *American Journal of Physical Anthropology* 81(4):545–554.

Brune, Gunnar

1975 Major and Historical Springs of Texas. Report 189. Austin: Texas Water Development Board.

Bryant, M. D.

1941 A Far Southwestern Occurrence of Pitymys in Texas. *Journal of Mammalogy* 22:202.

Bryant, Vaughn M., Jr.
1977 A 16,000 Year Pollen Record of Vegetation Change in Central Texas. *Palynology* 1:143–159.
Bryant, Vaughn M., Jr., and Harry J. Shafer
1977 The Late Quaternary Paleoenvironment of Texas: A Model for Archeologists. *Bulletin of the Texas Archeological Society* 48:1–25.
Buchanan, G. D., and R. V. Talmadge
1954 The Geographical Distribution of the Armadillo in the United States. *Texas Journal of Science* 6:142–150.
Charles, Douglas K., and Jane E. Buikstra
1983 Archaic Mortuary Sites in the Central Mississippi Drainage: Distribution, Structure, and Behavioral Implications. In *Archaic Hunters and Gatherers in the American Midwest.* Edited by James L. Phillips and James A. Brown. Pp. 117–145. New York: Academic Press.
Cohen, M. N., and G. J. Armelagos
1984 *Paleopathology at the Origins of Agriculture.* New York: Academic Press.
Collins, Michael B.
1970 On the Peopling of Hitzfelder Cave. *Bulletin of the Texas Archeological Society* 4:301–304.
1990 Personal communication concerning the provenience of dog material from Kincaid Shelter.
Colton, Harold S.
1970 The Aboriginal Southwestern Indian Dog. *American Antiquity* 35(2): 153–159.
Crane, C. J.
1982 Macrobotanical Analysis. In *Archaeological Investigations at the San Gabriel Reservoir District, Central Texas.* Vol. 2. Edited by T. R. Hays. Pp. 15-2–15-5. Denton: Institute of Applied Sciences, North Texas State University.
Dalquest, W. W., E. Roth, and F. Judd
1969 The Mammal Fauna of Schulze Cave, Edwards County, Texas. *Florida State Museum Biological Sciences* 13:205–276.
Davis, W. B.
1978 The Mammals of Texas. *Texas Parks and Wildlife Department Bulletin* 41:1–298.
Dewez, Michel C.
1974 New Hypotheses Concerning Two Engraved Bones from La Grotte de Remouchamps, Belgium. *World Archaeology* 5(3):337–345.
Dickel, David N., Peter D. Schulz, and Henry M. McHenry
1984 Central California: Prehistoric Subsistence Changes and Health. In *Paleopathology at the Origins of Agriculture.* Edited by M. N. Cohen and G. J. Armelagos. Pp. 439–461. New York: Academic Press.
Dillehay, T. D.
1974 Late Quaternary Bison Population Changes on the Southern Plains. *Plains Anthropologist* 10(65):180–196.
Duffen, William A.
1939 The Morhiss Mound, A South-Texas Site and Some of Its Implications.

Paper presented at the annual meeting of the Texas Archaeological and Paleontological Society, Abilene, Texas, 28 October. Paper on file at the Texas Archeological Research Laboratory, University of Texas at Austin.

Ellen, Roy
1988   Foraging, Starch Extraction, and the Sedentary Lifestyle in the Lowland Rainforest of Central Seram. In *Hunters and Gatherers*. Vol. 1. *History, Evolution, and Social Change*. Edited by Tim Ingold, David Riches, and James Woodburn. Pp. 117–134. Oxford: Berg Publishers.

Fazekas, I. G., and F. Kosa
1978   *Forensic Fetal Osteology*. Budapest: Akademiai Kiado.

Fenneman, Nevin M.
1938   *Physiography of Eastern United States*. New York: McGraw-Hill.

Givens, R. Dale
1968   A Preliminary Report on Excavation at Hitzfelder Cave. *Bulletin of the Texas Archeological Society* 38:47–50.

Goldstein, Lynne Gail
1980   *Mississippian Mortuary Practices: A Case Study of Two Cemeteries in the Lower Illinois Valley*. Archaeological Program Scientific Papers 4. Evanston: Northwestern University

Goodman, A., G. J. Armelagos, and J. C. Rose
1980   Enamel Hypoplasias as Indicators of Stress in Three Prehistoric Populations from Illinois. *Human Biology* 52:515–528.

Gordon, K. D.
1982   A Study of Microwear on Chimpanzee Molars: Implications for Dental Microwear Analysis. *American Journal of Physical Anthropology* 59:195–215.

Gould, F. M.
1975   *The Grasses of Texas*. College Station: Texas A&M University Press.

Graham, R. W.
1976   Friesenhahn Cave Revisited (A Glimpse of Central Texas 20,000 Years Ago). *Mustang* 18(5):1–7.

Griffen, W. B.
1969   *Culture Change and Shifting Populations in Central Northern Mexico*. Anthropological Papers 13. Tucson: University of Arizona Press.

Gunn, Joel
1977   Envirocultural System for Central Texas. In *Hop Hill: Culture and Climatic Change in Central Texas*. By Joel Gunn and Royce Mahula. Special Report 5. Pp. 257–276. San Antonio: Center for Archaeological Research, University of Texas at San Antonio.

Gunn, Joel, and Royce Mahula
1977   *Hop Hill: Culture and Climatic Change in Central Texas*. Special Report 5. San Antonio: Center for Archaeological Research, University of Texas at San Antonio.

Hafsten, Ulf
1961   Pleistocene Development of Vegetation and Climate in the Southern

High Plains as Evidenced by Pollen Analysis. In *Paleoecology of the Llano Estacado*. Publication No. 1. Fort Burgwin Research Center, Southern Methodist University.

Hall, G. D.
1981   *Allens Creek: A Study in the Cultural Prehistory of the Lower Brazos River Valley, Texas*. Research Report 61. Austin: Texas Archeological Survey, University of Texas.
1988   Long-Bone Implements from Some Prehistoric Sites in Texas: Functional Interpretations Based on Ethnographic Analogy. *Bulletin of the Texas Archeological Society* 59:157–176.
N.d.   A Perspective on the Prehistoric Cemeteries of Southeast Texas: Loma Sandia in the Regional Setting. Manuscript on file at the Texas Archeological Research Laboratory, University of Texas at Austin.

Hartnady, Philip, and Jerome C. Rose
1991   Abnormal Tooth-Loss Patterns among Archaic-Period Inhabitants of the Lower Pecos Region, Texas. In *Advances in Dental Anthropology*. Edited by M. A. Kelley and C. S. Larsen. Pp. 267–278. New York: Wiley-Liss.

Heaton, T. H. E.
1987   The 15N/14N Ratios of Plants in South Africa and Namibia: Relationship to Climate and Coastal/Saline Environments. *Oecologia* 74:236–246.

Hertz, Robert
1960   Contribution to the Study of the Collective Representation of Death. In *Death and the Right Hand*. Pp. 29–88. Glencoe, Ill.: Free Press.

Hester, Thomas R.
1971   Archeological Investigations at the La Jita Site, Uvalde County, Texas. *Bulletin of the Texas Archeological Society* 42:51–148.
1989   An Archeological Synthesis. In *From the Gulf to the Rio Grande: Human Adaptation in Central, South, and Lower Pecos Texas*. By T. R. Hester, S. L. Black, D. G. Steele, B. W. Olive, A. A. Fox, K. J. Reinhard, and L. C. Bement. Research Series Report 33. Pp. 115–128. Fayetteville: Arkansas Archeological Survey.

Highley, C. L., J. A. Huebner, J. H. Labadie, R. J. Leneave, and R. R. Harrison
1988   Salvage Archaeology at the Brandes Site (41AU55), Austin County, Texas. *La Tierra* 15(3):6–19.

Huebner, Jeffery A.
1991   Cactus for Dinner, Again! An Isotopic Analysis of Late Archaic Diet in the Lower Pecos Region of Texas. In *Papers on Lower Pecos Prehistory*. Edited by Solveig A. Turpin. Studies in Archeology 8. Austin: Texas Archeological Research Laboratory, University of Texas.

Hulbert, Richard C., Jr.
1984   Latest Pleistocene and Holocene Leporid Faunas from Texas: Their Composition, Distribution, and Climatic Implications. *Southwestern Naturalist* 29(2):197–210.

Jackson, A. T.
1930 Field notes on file at the Texas Archeological Research Laboratory, University of Texas at Austin.

Jirikowic, Christine
1990 The Political Implications of a Cultural Practice: A New Perspective on Ossuary Burial in the Potomac Valley. *North American Archaeologist* 11(4):353–373.

Johnson, LeRoy, Jr.
1964 *The Devil's Mouth Site: A Stratified Campsite at Amistad Reservoir, Val Verde County, Texas.* Archaeology Series 6. Austin: Department of Anthropology, University of Texas.

Johnson, LeRoy, Jr., Dee Ann Suhm, and Curtis D. Tunnell
1962 *Salvage Archeology of Canyon Reservoir: The Wunderlich, Footbridge, and Oblate Sites.* Bulletin 5. Austin: Texas Memorial Museum.

Kelley, J. C.
1947 The Cultural Affiliations and Chronological Position of the Clear Fork Focus. *American Antiquity* 13(2):97–109.
1959 The Desert Cultures and the Balcones Phase: Archaic Manifestations in the Southwest and Texas. *American Antiquity* 24:276–288.

King, Thomas F.
1978 Don't That Beat the Band? Nonegalitarian Political Organization in Prehistoric Central California. In *Social Archeology, Beyond Subsistence and Dating.* Edited by Charles L. Redman, William T. Langhorn, Jr., Mary Jane Berman, Nina M. Versaggi, Edward V. Curtin, and Jeffrey C. Wanser. New York: Academic Press.

Kroeber, A. L.
1927 Disposal of the Dead. *American Anthropologist* 29:308–315.

Krueger, Harold W., and Charles H. Sullivan
1984 Models for Carbon Isotope Fractionation between Diet and Bone. In *Stable Isotopes in Nutrition.* Edited by J. R. Turnlund and P. E. Johnson. Pp. 205–220. Washington, D.C.: ACS Symposium Series.

Lord, K. J.
1984 *The Zooarcheology of Hinds Cave (41VV456).* College Station: Department of Anthropology, Texas A&M University.

Luke, C. J.
1980 *Continuing Archeology on State Highway 16: The Shep Site (41KR109) and the Wounded Eye Site (41KR107).* Publications in Archeology. Austin: State Department of Highways and Public Transportation.

Lukowski, Paul D.
1988 *Archaeological Investigations at 41BX1, Bexar County, Texas.* Archaeological Survey Report 135. San Antonio: Center for Archaeological Research, University of Texas at San Antonio.

Lundelius, E. L., Jr.
1967 Late Pleistocene and Holocene Faunal History of Central Texas. In *Pleistocene Extinctions: The Search for a Cause.* Edited by P. S. Martin and H. E. Wirth. Pp. 288–319. New Haven: Yale University Press.

1974 The Last Fifteen Thousand Years of Faunal Change in North America. *Museum Journal* 15:141–160.

1986 Vertebrate Paleontology of the Balcones Fault Trend. In *The Balcones Escarpment*. Edited by P. Abbott and C. Woodruff, Jr. Pp. 41–50. San Antonio: Geological Society of America.

Marks, Murray K.

1991 Bioarcheological Analysis of Bering Sinkhole. Manuscript on file at the Texas Archeological Research Laboratory, University of Texas at Austin.

Marks, Murray K., J. C. Rose, and E. L. Buie

1988 Bioarcheology of Seminole Sink. In *Seminole Sink: Excavation of a Vertical Shaft Tomb, Val Verde County, Texas*. Compiled by Solveig A. Turpin. Memoir 22. Pp. 75–118. *Plains Anthropologist* 33(122): Part 2.

Martin, P. S.

1984 Prehistoric Overkill: The Global Model. In *Quaternary Extinctions: A Prehistoric Revolution*. Edited by P. S. Martin and R. G. Klein. Pp. 354–403. Tucson: University of Arizona Press.

Maruyama, Magoroh

1963 The Second Cybernetics: Deviation-Amplifying Mutual Causal Processes. *American Scientist* 51:164–179.

Massler, M., I. Schour, and H. Poncher

1941 Developmental Pattern of the Child as Reflected in the Calcification Pattern of the Teeth. *American Journal of Diseases of Children* 62:33–67.

McIntosh, Susan

1988 Letter report to Augie Bering identifying the human remains from the track hoe back dirt. Rice University. Copy in possession of author.

McKern, W. C.

1939 The Midwestern Taxonomic Method as an Aid to Archaeological Culture Study. *American Antiquity* 4:301–313.

Michaels, George H.

1987 A Description and Analysis of Early Postclassic Lithic Technology at Colha, Belize. M.A. thesis, Texas A&M University, College Station.

Neck, Raymond W.

1991 Marine, Freshwater, and Terrestrial Mollusks from the Bering Sinkhole (41KR241). Manuscript on file at the Texas Archeological Research Laboratory, University of Texas at Austin.

Nowak, Ronald M.

1979 *North American Quaternary Canis*. Monograph of the Museum of Natural History No. 6. Lawrence: University of Kansas.

Oldfield, Frank, and James Schoenwetter

1975 Discussion of the Pollen Analytical Evidence. In *Late Pleistocene Environments in the Southern High Plains*. Publication 9. Pp. 149–178. Dallas: Fort Burgwin Research Center, Southern Methodist University.

Olsen, Stanley J.

1974 Early Domestic Dogs in North America and Their Origins. *Journal of Field Archaeology* 1(3/4):343–345.

Pearce, J. E.
1919   Indian Mounds and Other Relics of Indian Life in Texas. *American Anthropologist* 21:223–245.
1932   The Present Status of Texas Archeology. *Bulletin of the Texas Archeological and Paleontological Society* 4:44–54.
Perino, G., and W. J. Bennett, Jr.
1978   Archaeological Investigations at the Mahaffey Site, Ch-1, Hugo Reservoir, Choctaw County, Oklahoma. Manuscript on file at the Museum of the Red River, Idabel, Oklahoma.
Prewitt, E. R.
1974   *Archeological Investigations at the Loeve-Fox Site, Williamson County, Texas.* Research Report 49. Austin: Texas Archeological Survey, University of Texas at Austin.
1976   The Rogers Springs Site: 1974 Investigations. Research Report 54. Unpublished manuscript, Texas Archeological Survey, University of Texas at Austin.
1981   Cultural Chronology in Central Texas. *Bulletin of the Texas Archeological Society* 52:65–89.
1982   Archeological Investigations at the Loeve-Fox and Loeve Tombstone Bluff Sites in the Granger Lake District of Central Texas. In *Archaeological Investigations at the San Gabriel Reservoir District, Central Texas.* Edited by T. R. Hays. Vol. 4. Denton: Institute of Applied Sciences, North Texas State University.
1985   From Circleville to Toyah: Comments on Central Texas Chronology. *Bulletin of the Texas Archeological Society* 54:201–238.
Reinhard, Karl J., Ben W. Olive, and D. Gentry Steele
1989   Bioarcheological Synthesis. In *From the Gulf to the Rio Grande: Human Adaptation in Central, South, and Lower Pecos, Texas.* By T. R. Hester, S. L. Black, D. G. Steele, B. W. Olive, A. A. Fox, K. J. Reinhard, and L. C. Bement. Pp. 129–140. Research Series No. 33. Fayetteville: Arkansas Acheological Survey.
Rose, Jerome C.
1984   Bioarcheology of the Cedar Grove Site. In *Cedar Grove.* Edited by W. F. Limp. Pp. 227–266. Research Series 23. Fayetteville: Arkansas Archeological Survey.
Rose, J. C., B. A. Burnett, M. Blaeuer, and M. S. Nassaney
1984   Paleopathology and the Origins of Maize Agriculture in the Lower Mississippi Valley and Caddoan Culture Areas. In *Paleopathology at the Origins of Agriculture.* Edited by M. N. Cohen and G. J. Armelagos. Pp. 393–424. New York: Academic Press.
Rose, J. C., K. W. Condon, and A. H. Goodman
1985   Diet and Dentition: Developmental Disturbances. In *The Analysis of Prehistoric Diets.* Edited by R. I. Gilert, Jr., and J. H. Meilke. Pp. 281–305. New York: Academic Press.
Rose, J. C., M. K. Marks, and E. B. Riddick
1983   Chapter 13: Bioarchaeology of the Bug Hill Site. In *Bug Hill: Excavation of a Multicomponent Midden Mound in the Jackfork Valley, Southeast Okla-*

homa. Pp. 241–278. Report of Investigations 81–1. Pollock, La.: New World Research.

Rosenberg, Robert

1985   The Mammalian Fauna of Seminole Sink. In *Seminole Sink: Excavation of a Vertical Shaft Tomb, Val Verde County, Texas*. Compiled by S. A. Turpin. Pp. 197–210. Research Report 93. Austin: Texas Archeological Survey, University of Texas.

Schaedel, Richard P.

1991   Personal communication concerning the use of the term "cemetery" in nonurban societies and the concept of cultural shrines.

Schmidly, David J.

1977   *The Mammals of Trans-Pecos Texas*. College Station: Texas A&M University Press.

Schoeninger, M. J., and M. J. DeNiro

1984   Nitrogen and Carbon Isotope Composition of Bone Collagen from Marine and Terrestrial Animals. *Geochimica et Cosmochimica Acta* 48:625–639.

Schulz, P. D.

1977   Task Activity and Anterior Tooth Grooving in Prehistoric California Indians. *American Journal of Physical Anthropology* 46:87–92.

Shafer, Harry J.

1963   Test Excavations at the Youngsport Site: A Stratified Terrace in Bell County, Texas. *Bulletin of the Texas Archeological Society* 34:57–81.

Shoup, Richard

1985   Burial Data from the Loma Sandia Site. Manuscript on file at the Texas Archeological Research Laboratory, University of Texas at Austin.

Sisson, Septimus, and James D. Grossman

1950   *The Anatomy of the Domestic Animals*. 3d ed. Philadelphia: W. B. Saunders Co.

Skinner, S. A.

1978   A Secondary Burial Cache from West Texas. *Journal of Field Archaeology* 5(4):484–490.

Skinner, S. A., H. Haas, and S. L. Wilson

1980   The Elcor Burial Cave: An Example of Public Archaeology from West Texas. *Plains Anthropologist* 25(87):1–15.

Slaughter, B. H.

1963   Some Observations Concerning the Genus Smilodon, with Special References to *Smilodon fatalis*. *Texas Journal of Science* 10:68–81.

Sorrow, William M., Harry J. Shafer, and Richard E. Ross

1967   *Excavations at Stillhouse Hollow Reservoir*. Papers of the Texas Archeological Salvage Project 11. Austin: Texas Archeological Salvage Project.

Stebbins, Robert C.

1966   A Field Guide to Western Reptiles and Amphibians. Boston: Houghton Mifflin.

Steele, D. Gentry, and Claud A. Bramblett

1988   *The Anatomy and Biology of the Human Skeleton*. College Station: Texas A&M University Press.

Stock, Janet A.
1983   The Prehistoric Diet of Hinds Cave (41VV456), Val Verde County, Texas: The Coprolite Evidence. M.A. thesis, Department of Anthropology, Texas A&M University.

Story, Dee Ann
1965   The Archeology of Cedar Creek Reservoir, Henderson and Kaufman Counties, Texas. *Bulletin of the Texas Archeological Society* 36:163–257.

Stuiver, M., and G. Pearson
1986   A Computer Program for Radiocarbon Dates. *Radiocarbon* 28:805–838.

Suhm, D. A.
1960   A Review of Central Texas Archeology. *Bulletin of the Texas Archeological Society* 29:63–108.

Suhm, D. A., A. D. Krieger, and E. B. Jelks
1954   An Introductory Handbook of Texas Archeology. *Bulletin of the Texas Archeological Society* 25.

Taylor, A. J., and C. L. Highley
N.d.   Archaeological Investigations at the Loma Sandia Site (41LK28): A Prehistoric Cemetery and Campsite in Live Oak County, Texas. Manuscript in preparation for the State Department of Highways and Public Transportation, Austin.

Taylor, Walter W.
1948   *A Study of Archeology*. American Anthropological Association Memoir Series 69. *American Anthropologist* 50(3): Part 2.

Toomey, Richard S., III.
1990   Faunal Evidence for a Middle Holocene Dry Period in Central Texas— Hall's Cave. Paper presented at the annual meeting of the Geological Society of America, Dallas.

Turner, Ellen S., and Thomas R. Hester
1985   *A Field Guide to Stone Artifacts of Texas Indians*. Austin: Texas Monthly Press.

Turnlund, Judith R., and Phyllis E. Johnson
1984   *Stable Isotopes in Nutrition*. ACS Symposium Series. Washington, D.C.: American Chemical Society.

Turpin, Solveig A. (Compiler)
1988   *Seminole Sink: Excavation of a Vertical Shaft Tomb, Val Verde County, Texas*. Memoir 22. *Plains Anthropologist* 33(122):1–156.
1992   More about Mortuary Practices in the Lower Pecos River Region of Southwest Texas. *Plains Anthropologist* 37:7–17.

Turpin, Solveig A., and Leland C. Bement
1988   The Site and Its Setting. In *Seminole Sink: Excavation of a Vertical Shaft Tomb, Val Verde County, Texas*. Compiled by Solveig A. Turpin. Memoir 22. *Plains Anthropologist* 33(122):1–18.

Turpin, Solveig A., M. Henneberg, and D. H. Riskind
1986   Late Archaic Mortuary Practices of the Lower Pecos River Region, Southwest Texas. *Plains Anthropologist* 31(114):295–315.

Ubelaker, D. H., W. Phenice, and W. M. Bass
1969   Artificial Interproximal Grooving of the Teeth in American Indians. *American Journal of Physical Anthropology* 30:145–150.

Weir, Frank A.

1967 The Greenhaw Site: A Burned-Rock Midden Cluster of the Edwards Plateau Aspect. Unpublished M.A. thesis, University of Texas at Austin.

1976 The Central Texas Archaic. Unpublished Ph.D. dissertation, Washington State University, Pullman.

Wilson, Ernest W.

1930 Burned Rock Mounds of Southwest Texas. *Bulletin of the Texas Archeological and Paleontological Society* 2:59–63.

Winans, Milissa

1989 Personal communication concerning the statistical overlap in dental metrics of woodrat species.

Wingate, R. J., and T. R. Hester

1972 Ten Burials from Green Lake, Texas. *Florida Anthropologist* 25(3):119–127.

Woodburn, James

1982 Social Dimensions of Death in Four African Hunting and Gathering Societies. In *Death and the Regeneration of Life*. Edited by M. Bloch and J. Parry. Pp. 187–211. Cambridge: Cambridge University Press.

Wright, T., and E. L. Lundelius, Jr.

1963 *Post-Pleistocene Raccoons from Central Texas and Their Zoogeographic Significance*. The Pearce-Sellards Series 2. Austin: Texas Memorial Museum, University of Texas.

Young, Diane

1985 The Paleoindian Skeletal Material from Horn Rock Shelter in Central Texas. *Current Research in the Pleistocene* 2:39–40.

Index